Praise for *Home Behind the Sun*

"*Home Behind the Sun* is so elegant and moving that it nearly took my breath away. The prose glimmers and rattles and nearly every page forced me to wrestle with important questions about joy, whimsy, imagination, and purpose. *Home Behind the Sun* is a poetic portrait of God's glory that is as brave as it is beautiful. As you read, breathe deeply."

—JONATHAN MERRITT, AUTHOR OF *JESUS IS BETTER THAN YOU IMAGINED*

"I'm convicted by the precise reflections and tempered provocations my dear friends, Jason Locy and Timothy Willard, deliver in *Home Behind the Sun*. Put this book on your coffee table and read one chapter each weekend. You will see what I mean. A brilliant exposé of what really matters in life, just when it seemed we were about to forget."

—GABE LYONS, FOUNDER OF Q AND AUTHOR OF *THE NEXT CHRISTIANS*

"In *Home Behind the Sun*, Jason Locy and Timothy Willard show us how to let the brilliance of God's presence shine through every nook and cranny of our lives. This book is a cool drink of water on a hot day for busy leaders who don't stop enough to consider God's glory; I highly recommend it."

—JOSHUA DUBOIS, BEST-SELLING AUTHOR OF
THE PRESIDENT'S DEVOTIONAL; FORMER DIRECTOR,
WHITE HOUSE FAITH-BASED INITIATIVE

"Jason and Tim write with such convicted honesty, you'll pause midsentence to reflect. They stir our imaginations toward a brilliant life, with a gracious exposure to the blind spots in each of us."

—REBEKAH LYONS, AUTHOR OF *FREEFALL TO FLY*

"*Home Behind the Sun* is a beautiful, intelligent, weighty collection. I loved it, and I can't wait to share it with people who, like me, like nothing better than to lose themselves in graceful language and find themselves in resounding themes."

—SHAUNA NIEQUIST, AUTHOR OF *BREAD & WINE*

"Few authors possess the gift of transporting readers into otherworldly regions, far away from the din and clamor this planet offers. In *Home Behind the Sun*, Tim and Jason serve as your tour guides, weaving their words, to lead you down unexplored pathways. Through your journeys, you'll discover a rich and robust Faith—the answer to your homesickness you've felt from the very beginning."

—KARY OBERBRUNNER, AUTHOR OF *DAY JOB TO DREAM JOB* AND CEO OF IGNITING SOULS AND REDEEM THE DAY

"To a crazy busy, on-the-go generation, my friends Tim and Jason offer upside-down advice: stop, reflect, wait on God. With masterful storytelling, the authors call us to see where our identity truly lies. *Home Behind the Sun* reminds us we are part of a greater story than we ever dreamed or imagined."

—PETER GREER, PRESIDENT AND CEO OF HOPE INTERNATIONAL AND AUTHOR OF *THE SPIRITUAL DANGER OF DOING GOOD*

"*Home Behind the Sun* is an act of obedience to God's call to 'tell of his wonderful acts.' It's a shout of worship, 'Thank you Lord!' It reminds me of David's words of thanksgiving and charge to us all to sing praises to God, to speak of all his wonders. Authors Timothy and Jason have helped convince me that more than ever I am to live as a happy living *doer* of the Word of God and not an exploitative hearer only."

—ANDREW PALAU, INTERNATIONAL EVANGELIST AND AUTHOR OF *THE SECRET LIFE OF A FOOL*

CONNECT WITH GOD

HOME

IN THE BRILLIANCE

BEHIND

OF THE EVERYDAY

the SUN

Timothy Willard and *Jason Locy*

NELSON
BOOKS

An Imprint of Thomas Nelson

Published in Nashville, Tennessee, by Nelson Books, an imprint of Thomas Nelson. Nelson Books and Thomas Nelson are registered trademarks of HarperCollins Christian Publishing, Inc.

Published in association with the literary agency of Christopher Ferebee, Norco, California.

Thomas Nelson titles may be purchased in bulk for educational, business, fund-raising, or sales promotional use. For information, please e-mail SpecialMarkets@ ThomasNelson.com.

Unless otherwise noted Scripture quotations are taken from the ENGLISH STANDARD VERSION. © 2001 by Crossway Bibles, a division of Good News Publishers.

Scripture quotations marked MSG are taken from *The Message* by Eugene H. Peterson. © 1993, 1994, 1995, 1996, 2000, 2001, 2002. Used by permission of NavPress Publishing Group. All rights reserved.

Scripture quotations marked KJV are taken from the KING JAMES VERSION.

Scripture quotations marked NLT are taken from the *Holy Bible*, New Living Translation. © 1996, 2004, 2007 by Tyndale House Foundation. Used by permission of Tyndale House Publishers, Inc., Carol Stream, Illinois 60188. All rights reserved.

Scripture quotations marked NIV are taken from the Holy Bible, New International Version®, NIV®. Copyright © 1973, 1978, 1984, 2011 by Biblica, Inc.® Used by permission of Zondervan. All rights reserved worldwide. www.zondervan.com

The Library of Congress Cataloging-in-Publication Data is on file with the Library of Congress.

ISBN: 978-1-4002-0566-0

Printed in the United States of America

14 15 16 17 18 RRD 6 5 4 3 2 1

For our daughters

Contents

CONTENTS

We all walk the long road.

—PEARL JAM

Prologue

THE BRILLIANCE OF HOME

When we let a mutual friend read the first draft of this book, he made an interesting comment: "I love how you guys are reframing the whole *imago Dei* discussion. I often feel like 'the image of God' gets narrowed into social justice compartments. If I'm not active in some cause, then I'm not fulfilling the gospel. Isn't it gospel living to raise my four boys and to make a living, supporting my wife and family?"

His comments caused us to shape the book into what you see now. We're passionate about God, and we're passionate about his world and what we can do as his followers in this world. But the gospel of Christ extends into *every* facet of this life. This is how we stumbled onto the concept of the brilliance of God's glory.

At first we discussed God's glory in terms of beauty. We had myriad discussions about the places in life where we saw beauty: in deformity, in innocence, in forgiveness, in physicality, in our work, in our relationships. It was an invisible type of beauty. And always we saw it contrasted with shadows—the afflictions of life.

But then we thought on beauty's source, and found ourselves wandering into God's brilliance. God's brilliance overwhelms the shadows of life. His brilliance fills us, through the Holy Spirit. And it's for God's brilliance, his glory, that we live and breathe and have our being. This simple but beautiful truth overwhelmed us.

When we sense God's brilliance in this life, we sense his glory, we sense *him*. It's why you feel strangely at home when you run into goodness and beauty, like when a friend sacrifices time in his or her day to help you, or when you find yourself exhilarated when you accomplish something great in your work or study.

But shadows remain. Daily we war with our own hearts, pushing down the hurt, pain, disillusionment, disappointment, bitterness, and betrayal. God's brilliance, however, compels us *through* the shadows. We long for it.

We all want something more in this life. Though in our wanting we often fall prey *to* the wanting. It's the difference between our longings moving us toward a beautiful and heavenly destination, and our longings ensnaring us, trapping us in the "teeth of our own lusts," as C. S. Lewis put it.

But Christ offers us that something more: *himself*. The Bible describes Christ as light, radiance, brilliance. In Christ, our longings become his longings and they look less shadowy and more like goodness and hope, love and delight—all the things that make this life feel like home.

Being at home is being *in* him. It's him dressing us in his brilliance, full of mystery and wonder, as you'd imagine exists behind the sun. When you look up on a sunny day and squint into the sunlight, do you ever wonder what lies behind it? Another world perhaps?

More color than you could ever imagine? The magic of the stars? Or simply, more of the brilliance.

As a child of God made in his image (*imago Dei*), you shine like the sun, or at least you should. We all should.

Is the world squinting into our brilliance? Do they encounter the healing and beauty, the hope and the glory of Christ *in* you? In us?

In writing this book we found ourselves on a journey into brilliance, finding clues to it along the way—forgiveness leading to reconciliation, beauty in the invisible, innocence conquering cynicism. We assembled this collection of essays as our field guide and now offer it to you. We invite you along as we journey home, behind the sun.

Tim and Jason

October 10, 2013

Oxford and Brooklyn

The sweetest thing in all my life has been the longing . . .
to find the place where all the beauty came from.

—C. S. LEWIS, *TILL WE HAVE FACES*

Chapter 1

We, the Brilliance Makers

WHY GOD'S GLORY SHOULD AFFECT
EVERY ASPECT OF OUR LIVES

In thy light shall we see light.
—DAVID THE PSALMIST

*Do you know I don't know how one can walk by a tree and not be happy
at the sight of it? How can one talk to a man and not be happy in loving
him! Oh, it's only that I'm not able to express it . . . And what beautiful
things there are at every step, that even the most hopeless man must feel
to be beautiful! Look at a child! Look at God's sunrise! Look at the
grass, how it grows! Look at the eyes that gaze at you and love you!*
—FYODOR DOSTOYEVSKY, *THE IDIOT*

I bring my heart to you, Light that teaches truth.
—SAINT AUGUSTINE

I (Tim) am on my way to meet my friends. The winter sky shapes my thoughts, affecting my mood and dazzling my eyes. It's as if someone with a sharpened No. 2 pencil is carving bare deciduous limbs into the bitter-cold rising canvas: green, now purple, indigo, and blue. The pencil scratches the tree-line horizon into the unfolding sunrise.

The smell from the steaming cup rattling in the holder to my right churns the ever-diminishing vapor of my morning mind. I am groggy; the coffee helps.

The pencil flecks are brushed, smeared even into the frame, and the glow of the morning quickens their silhouettes into wonder-smeared conifers against the stark ridgeline. Blasted sleep blurs and burns my eyes. It's too quiet to think out loud, so I keep everything in my head. I assemble the pieces of the horizon as they sneak past the trees into the open sky. The cold hurts my fingers gripping the wheel. No matter, I'll be there soon.

Blink, blink, blink. Three lights flicker on in the farm to my right; a stone house amid the barns and silos yawns, simmering with morning food, tossing blankets, and crackling wood.

And from the wood the smoke rises and smears its own shade into the frame augmenting the night fading to day, fading into life. Just to the right of Polaris sits the bright moon, the pale sliver hanging beside this dream and that. All is waking.

Over the river and through the woods, the hill, the bend, the here and after. I approach the end of my drive to the diner and listen to the pencil scratching, the rubbing, the smearing, the crackling, the sipping, the lovemaking, and the cries of the all-encompassing morning.

Just then, when the staccato of my groggy mind eases to the alle-gro rise of the blasting sun, I stop shivering and warm to the music all around. It's as if I'm witnessing the Creation moments all rolled into one. Let there be light. Let there be day. Let there be you, and let there be me.

As I wait for my friends, amid this chaotic symphony of morning-rise silence, I hear Eliot's whimper and Psyche's sister[1] and remember that life and death, pain and pride, and all the shadows of life rise together. I remember the cunning serpent. "You shall surely not die," he said. "You are gods." We believed him and walked into the shadows.

Even on this day of days, this sleight-of-hand time of non-chalance and banter, the shadows rise with us all and seep into charcoal smears of stick-figure carvings of winter's barren trees. They enter the frame and sour. They are like trolls, boiling us slowly and gorging on our flesh.

Yet I am not dismayed or weakened by the presence of shadows. On the contrary, I think out loud of the stories I know of heroes and villains, of music I love—major key and bright, minor key and sad, of people I know—decent and decadent. How extravagant these things make life, this fugue-like tension of point and counterpoint. Every day it is there, and it is undeniable.

I'm on time and already sipping my second cup of coffee when the others arrive.

At breakfast we sit with our own agendas: inquiry, testing, obli-gation, love, and need. The diner coffee isn't so friendly. It's weak but hot, and it draws us closer to the table, to our mugs, and to each other. The day heaves as we exchange laughter, smiles, and glances at mobile phones, etcetera, etcetera.

Here comes the hurry. Off we go now to nowhere and to no one in particular.

***

Buckle up. That's me driving in the middle of the canvas. Heading home to work to catch a glimpse of the morning brilliance in another fragment of the day. As I make the return trip on the back roads zigzagging the cornfields, a quiet chorus lifts as the day stretches full-blown. It is the chorus of the invisible, the chorus of the brilliance, the meaning behind the waking gesture, the waiting brilliance behind the colors and trees and people. It is the chorus of God's glory.

I can almost hear him say, "It was good. It was very good."

The chorus breathes life to the canvas of shadows. If it were a song sung by human voice, it would sound like the *Sanctus*:

> Holy, holy, holy Lord God of hosts.
>
> The heavens and earth are full of your glory.
>
> Hosanna in the highest.
>
> Blessed is the one who comes in the name of the Lord.
>
> Hosanna in the highest.[2]

Holy, holy, holy, "awe inspiring God of Heaven." You are transcendent. Hosanna in the highest, "humble indwelling divinity of Jesus the Messiah."[3] You are immanent. All creation resounds in worship like the tabernacle it is. For we encounter God within himself, Creator within creation. That is why I long for you, God. Your goodness eclipses the shadows, my shadows. I stammer and choke because

I feel I am caught in a place for which I was not made. Yet you equip me to hum the chorus, to carry your brilliance—a shadow chaser.

The angels cry "Holy" again and again. The morning cries it as well. And though life bends to the shadows, I cry it too. Pull me close to the aloof gestures and distant eyes of those who need me. Pull me close to your righteous gesture and deep eyes; paint and repaint the canvas for me each morning so that I may hear the chorus of your beauty, of your brilliance.

Who will not fear you, O Lord, and bring glory to your name?

GOD'S BRILLIANCE

The early-morning drive kindled friendships and a worshipful reflection that jump-started my day. These moments reflected God's brilliance, his glory, into the very fabric of my life. The shining remnants of heaven we see here on earth draw us closer to him.

You see the brilliance, don't you? You saw it this morning when you woke at the ungodly hour and poured your coffee as the sun backlit your front windows.

You saw it in your friend's face when you met to chat before class. She appreciated your honest words. She drank in your "I'm sorry. Forgive me?"

You felt it yesterday when you finished that project you thought would never end. What joy you found. What satisfaction. A bit of God's glory? Yes, his brilliance brimmed in that soul pocket of yours.

But God's brilliance is more than the *thing* we sense behind the beautiful things we see or the redemptive feelings we experience in our relationships. *It's him. It's his being.* It's only by his brilliance that we see all that is true, all that is good, and all that is beautiful. Like C. S. Lewis, I believe in Christianity, just as "I believe that the Sun has risen, not only because I see it, but because by it I see everything else."[4]

"In thy light shall we see light," wrote the psalmist.[5] And we do see the light because we are born from the light. We are, in fact, his brilliant ones. We walk in his brilliance, and by this brilliance we see the world anew. We believe in him and pass from blindness into light, "our lives gradually becoming brighter and more beautiful as God enters our lives and we become like him."[6]

But do we live *in* the brilliance? The popular Christian culture teeters close to a social gospel when it focuses the gospel message on justice and mercy and leaves out the motivation of love and affection from which our actions originate. It isn't enough to pursue justice when we have not pursued an honest and intimate relationship with Jesus. No doubt grace befriends effort, but when our efforts turn to *earning*, we no longer live within a gospel framework. We cannot truly love any other human with our works and effort until we learn to love God.

For me, worship (or the lack of it) testifies to the depth of my love for God and the true luminosity of the brilliance in which I walk. Worship operates as a litmus test for my spiritual affections.

WHERE DO MY AFFECTIONS LIE?

I sat with several friends—musicians and worship leaders all—in a basement. We spent the evening in quiet prayer and song giving to God. Spontaneous prayers emanated as several players picked and keyed. I sat with my eyes closed and listened.

I didn't want to leave. It was as if Jesus had walked among us, sat down, and picked up a guitar so he could contribute. I find my soul yearning for such times more often. I'd rather sit with friends in quiet worship than consume entertainment. I'd rather walk in the woods with him than busy myself with, well, busyness.

And do not think I'm describing an experience brought on by emotion. Yes, emotion is part of it; God evokes our deepest emotions when we draw close to him. It is a by-product of standing in his presence. We fall down as dead like John the Beloved before the Shining One in that dazzling Revelation scene.[7] But what draws me to God is God himself.

For me, worship through song and prayer and contemplation acts as a vehicle. I close my eyes and in a mysteriously real way am transported into his holy presence. If I'm able to cut through the noise of the morning, the noise of stress, and the noise of my thoughts, I can, in my mind's eye, stand before God.

If I define *worship* as giving worth to him, then worship can mirror the gospel in that we proclaim God's worth through music and song and we live it daily in acts of service and love. And God is the center of that worth giving.

Think about what you sing to God when you worship him in song. Think about what you do during your day to ascribe him glory. Why these words and songs? Why these acts? Because you love him. Your affection for him motivates you to worship him with your whole life—through song, through prayer, through contemplation and just acts. We worship God because we, like Paul the apostle, forsake everything to *know* him. At least we try, right?

And who is the God we know? Why does he draw us to himself?

What about him endears our affections and motivates our worship? We love and worship God because of who he is.

Because God is beautiful. The concept of beauty vexes even the greatest minds. From Aristotle to Aquinas to Lewis, we fall at the feet of the beautiful. Some say that beauty demands form first—that we must behold something in order to know beauty exists. Others remind us that the forms of beauty we behold point to something else, the thing *behind* the thing. It's not really the thing we desire at all. We see beauty, and we long for God.[8]

Because God is good. When we say God is good, we describe his being: "in him we live and move and have our being."[9] The early church apologist Athenagoras affirmed, "Goodness is so much a part of God that, without it, he could not exist."[10] His goodness creates for us a moral origin; pain and suffering shatter against this perfect morality. No matter how much they rise to conquer us, God overwhelms them, causing good to come from even the blackest circumstances. This is who we worship, our *good* God.

Because God is truth. Truth, as J. I. Packer put it, "is a quality of persons" before it is something that can be proved or disproved.[11] Packer, of course, is speaking of God's qualities. We inherit truth from God because he *is* truth. Augustine said, "'Your law is truth' (Ps. 118:142) and truth is you (John 14:6)."[12] We receive God's moral stamp of truth when we enter the world and live as ambassadors of his truth, which is rooted in his very being. It's that shard of moral purity stuck in our souls that frustrates us so much. It wars inside us our whole lives.

When we close our eyes and find ourselves transported during our church gatherings to the throne room of God, this is the God we worship. He is altogether beautiful. He is altogether good. He is altogether truth.

When we step from the church building and into our everyday lives, when we begin our mornings in quiet and then move to serve our friends, our spouses, or our coworkers, when we sit down for coffee with a friend in order to work through a problem that demands forgiveness—these are our spiritual acts of worship. This is the God we worship. He is altogether beautiful. He is altogether good. He is altogether truth.

And it is this "all of him," this beauty, this goodness, and this truth, that we encounter in the everyday. They constitute his brilliance. When we center our lives on him, his glory follows. It shapes us, and with it, we shape the world.

WE, THE BRILLIANCE MAKERS

From all of him, we find our being, we find our truth, we find our goodness, and we find our beauty. Maybe this is what the apostle Paul means when he says we move from glory to glory.[13] God's glory, his brilliance, persists throughout the universe and finds its way into us.

It leaks from us as we walk through life. It's like the story of the women from India who, with cracked jars, carried water back to the village. The trail eventually becomes a path of flowers as the water leaks from the vessels. Imagine the beauty from a life marked by the motivation of love leaking within relationships and work and pain and victory. When we live to bring God glory above all else, his glory, in turn, leaks from our lives in ways we cannot fathom.

His brilliance paints our world with its invisible hues. We see those hues in the lives and character of our family members and friends. We see the very same hues emerge from the shadowy places of pain, suffering, and death. For some people the shadowy parts of life are more visible and more of a reality than the beautiful parts, and as they grow, nothing glows as it once did. Life seems to tread onward in pale tones.

If we follow the line of beauty, it points to God's brilliance, for he is the source of goodness—for he alone is good.[14] And that goodness manifests itself within each one of us. "Your creation has its being from the fullness of your goodness," declared Saint Augustine.[15] It is the measuring line we use when we see a sunset and gasp, "How beautiful!" Beauty that is good, beauty that is true, points to our very existence as human beings, and our existence points to the Creator. If beauty comes from God, then all life's affliction is eclipsed by his glory,[16] his profound goodness. What would people live like if they lived in the profundity of God's invisible line of beauty?

In the following pages you will find this God of brilliance in unseen beauty, in innocence, in forgiveness, and in affliction. You will see how God's brilliance overwhelms the shadows, eclipsing the brutality of a world fallen to pieces. You will find brilliance in your work, in your love for friends and family.

You will need to squint as you read because God cracks through it all, doesn't he? And so we stand with you in the midst of the broken pieces of our world, and we cry for hope. But it's not a weepy cry. It's a crying out—a shout of praise, a song of worship. That we once rebelled but now we run to you, the Crushing One, the Brilliant One.

As Christians, if we believe our lives become more and more like Christ's on a daily basis, and if we believe his glory shines through us, how should we live? To be a *Brilliance Maker* means to live differently. It requires a motivation of deep affection for God coupled with the by-products of that affection: beautiful efforts. For parents, it involves the everyday grind of working and child rearing, of educating and discipling. For married couples, it's striving to mimic a biblical model of love and sacrifice. For singles, in a search for purpose in our work and calling. It means we are not trapped by the temporal; instead we are free to live within a heavenly perspective.

We live out the brilliance.

We counter perversion with truth.

We combat despair with joy.

We topple bitterness and resentment with forgiveness.

We eliminate cynicism with belief and whimsy.

We erase perversion with purity.

We overcome pain with healing.

We offer the brilliance.

We are the Brilliance Makers.

Chapter 2

Brutalized

TRUE CHRISTIAN FREEDOM IS FOUND IN OUR WILLINGNESS TO BE LIFE GIVERS

Most of the shadows of life are caused by standing in our own sunshine.
—RALPH WALDO EMERSON

Come away, O human child!
To the waters and the wild
With a faery, hand in hand,
For the world's more full of weeping than you can understand.
—W. B. YEATS

We stumble and fall constantly even when we are most enlightened. But when we are in true spiritual darkness, we do not even know that we have fallen.
—THOMAS MERTON

When prominent magazines resort to plastering sexed-up ten-year-olds on their pages to lure readers, we know fashion culture has fallen from high class to no class. Yet that's what happened when *French Vogue* featured Thylane Lena-Rose Blondeau striking sultry poses in provocative clothes in its December 2010 issue. Readers, including the progressive French, winced.

Next, French fashion brand Jours Après Lunes launched a new line of "loungerie," a hybrid of lounge clothing and lingerie that a four-year-old can wear. Jours Après Lunes's new line not only marks a new standard for fashion but also raises the bar in the sexualization of women. Backers of the new sexed-up adolescent line praised its cute factor. Critics said the fashion company stepped over the line.

But this is nothing new. In 1999, Calvin Klein scratched plans for a billboard in Times Square depicting two six-year-old boys wearing nothing but their underwear while standing on a sofa and arm wrestling. Then in 2003, Abercrombie & Fitch came under fire for its XXX catalog. The pages contained images of nudity to near orgies. The models? Young adults. A&F's penchant for exploiting young people continued when in the spring of 2011, the company launched a line of push-up bras for girls as young as seven.

What does it say about our society when we're willing to place unwitting children in sexy clothing to sell underwear? But more important, what message are we communicating to our little ones about self-worth and personal beauty? The beauty of innocence is replaced by the allure of the hypersexualized.

A study published in the September 2011 issue of *Sexuality and Culture* sheds light on what many of us already know. University of Buffalo researchers compiled more than one thousand images from forty years of *Rolling Stone* magazine, comparing male and female poses, wardrobe, and language used in the articles. The study showed that women have been vastly more sexualized than men. In the 2000s there was a marked increase in hypersexualization of women in the magazine, which is regarded as a pop culture barometer.

Hypersexualization refers to images that communicate to the reader that the person in the image desires sex. Sociologist Erin Hatton said, "We don't necessarily think it's problematic for women to be portrayed as 'sexy.' But we do think it is problematic when nearly all images of women depict them not simply as 'sexy women' but as passive objects for someone else's sexual pleasure."[1]

According to Haden, the hypersexualization of women increases violence against women and girls, sexual harassment, and antiwomen attitudes among men and boys, not to mention the proliferation of eating disorders and general body dissatisfaction. And one can't help shuddering at the implications of a society that shuns human trafficking on the one hand but applauds provocative young "professionals" for profit on the other.

In this hypersexualized framework, young girls become mere objects. The ads begin the erotic process of tearing down their humanity and building up sex icons. With each flip of the magazine page or click of the mouse, we move young girls and women closer to a world of abuse, disorder, and rape.

ANNIHILATING OURSELVES

Philosopher Hannah Arendt said that given the chance and left unchecked, our modern advanced society would annihilate itself.[2] In a world bent on consuming information, images, artifacts, and yes, even people, we daily partake in the feeding frenzy of our unrestrained society, making Arendt's world of self-annihilation seem normative.

Western society touts sexuality as a defining element of our humanity; to suppress it would be unnatural. Morality issues stand as the main challenges with which the church must contend in the secular age. Some, such as pastor Timothy Keller, regard the lapse of morality in our culture as one of the primary daggers thrust at the heart of truth as well as a primary hindrance to church revival.[3] Indeed, God created us as sexual beings, but our sexuality should be stewarded with discernment. Here we offer mere critique on our culture but, desiring to see God's brilliance revive the church and our nation, we hold the mirror of truth up to ourselves, the church. Are we stewarding the beauty of sex and relationships in a way that draws a watching world to us?

When we wield sexuality from an individualistic point of view, we end up not only hurting ourselves but also those in society we should protect: children.

Theologian J. I. Packer said "sexual laxity" does not make a person more human. Rather, it "brutalizes" an individual. God designed us to run on and be satisfied with *soulish* things. "As rational persons," he wrote, "we were made to bear God's moral image— that is, our souls were made to 'run' on the practice of worship,

law-keeping, truthfulness, honesty, discipline, self-control, and service to God and our fellows."[4]

When we live contrary to our designed purpose, we dry up and
lose the capacity for shame. As a result, those soulish things inside
us diminish. And when our souls diminish, the glory within us dims
as well. We muck around like brutes, dehumanized and spiritually
dead.

If we dig beneath the surface, we find the incessant drive for
sexual fulfillment and even sexual violence stems from despair—
that place where sin makes man his own lawmaker, where meaning
dissipates. From this despairing perspective philosopher Friedrich
Nietzsche's quip "Man is an end" sounds apropos.[5] Life holds no
meaning. God is dead, so let's do as we see fit.

We know Nietzsche's terminus idea of humanity veers off the
road of truth. In fact, the gospel paints sex and life with vibrant
meaning and inherent goodness. God created us *from* Love (the
community of himself, his being) in order *to* love—a glory-giving
purpose and existence to be sure. To live means to think and act
with a heavenly purpose and a heavenly directive. We are children
of the light and to be such demands not only to believe life has
meaning founded upon the truth of God himself but also to live
within that meaning.

The early Christian thinkers regarded God as light and being.
Darkness, they believed, was nonbeing. In a somewhat comical simile
they described those who think they live in darkness to be people who
face the sunlight and yet shut their eyes tight, all the while thinking darkness exists where no darkness can prevail. There they stand

before the all-consuming light who *is* God, closing their eyes as if to wish away his existence and their own:

> This is the crisis we're in: God-light streamed into the world, but men and women everywhere ran for the darkness. They went for the darkness because they were not really interested in pleasing God. Everyone who makes a practice of doing evil, addicted to denial and illusion, hates God-light and won't come near it, fearing a painful exposure. But anyone working and living in truth and reality welcomes God-light so the work can be seen for the God-work it is.[6]

The more we turn from light to darkness, the more the dark consumes our beings, the more brutish we become. We are in fact brutes, like Tolkien's unforgettable character Gollum fascinated with his precious. Our precious becomes the enslavement to the body's desires. We do not realize that in our self-obsession, if we looked in the mirror we would see only the reflection of a brute, a hideous distortion of the image we were created to be.

Previously we discussed how love motivates our worship. God draws us even as we pursue him through glory giving. We pursue his essence, his being, and we find his being full of truth and goodness and beauty. "Truth is a person."[7] And that person is Christ, "the radiance of God's glory."[8] Would we rather be a reflection of the radiance of Christ or see the reflection of a brute, distorted and disfigured, darkened by death, filthy inside and out? Are we caught in the frivolous tension of always reaching for more but becoming less and less?

WE'RE BRUTES TOO

We see in the Jours Après Lunes's loungerie subtle lines of despair, a pervading darkness extending into all corners of culture. The world and even some Christians walk around with eyes shut tight, stumbling into untruth. The writer Frederick Buechner published a sermon in which he talked about a fantastic hope that someday Jesus would return and rescue us, the broken rebels, from this shadowy pursuit.

Hope alone, he said, reigns as our triumph-virtue. For though love marks the Christian, hope draws the world unto love. Peter Kreeft observed, "Hope means that our heads do not bump up against the low ceiling of this world; hope means that the exhilarating, wonderful, and terrifying winds of Heaven blow in our ears."[9]

But who is to say the Christian culture looks or acts any different than the pop culture in all its pornified glory? In his sermon Buechner also suggested we must be willing to be fantastic in our cultural engagement because "Christ himself was fantastic."[10] After all, he was the nomad Messiah who established his ministry upon the practice of flipping the cultural norm. He took the brutish and made it vibrant. He stooped to raise the whore from her dusty shame. He invited the bludgeoned thief to paradise. He wept over death and shook off his disdain for it and our lack of trust like a horse snorting and shaking his mane in defiance.

The French fashionistas show us a most hideous and overt example of the brutalization of humankind—a hungering dark, unrelenting and vicious. But we must wake every morning and face this brutishness and contend for the faith.

We're not tasked to navigate shadows. We're tasked to shine as a bright city on a hill—a gleaming beacon of hope. Has our light dimmed?

IN OUR OWN CAMP

We cannot underestimate the importance of language. Again we look to Buechner's sermon and find his exultation to use the language of the culture. We must speak the language of the people, he contended. We must use technology and paper and magazines and all the mediums at our disposal to bring hope to a darkling world.

We must communicate with common words and common mediums. Every one of us can write words and make sentences, but the writers among us take those words and sentences, form ideas and stories, and publish books. We can argue all day about the medium being the message and all that. But we don't have all day. We have right now to determine what language we, as Christians, are to speak to this shadowy world.

In our book *Veneer* we suggest the language of culture is less about the use of the tools of technology and more about the meaning communicated through our consumptive mind-set, mimicking the celebrity culture and failing to steward progress in a way that glorifies God. If we can agree on this definition of the *language of culture*, then we dare not attempt to speak it. And yet, that's what we find ourselves doing. When a popular pastor, "thought leader," or "celebrity blogger" says something via a book, a blog, or a conference presentation, we must make our opinions heard—airing our disdain in our own social media fiefdoms for the world to see. Those actions leave little distinction between our Christian discourse and that of the bickering heads on cable news or the cynical celebrity gossip columnists.

We watch, we skim, we post, we stir the blogosphere—our

new means of burning our so-called heretics. The Internet provides everyone with a voice. The larger the platform the louder the voice. Too often Christians, in an effort to gain a seat at the cultural table, sacrifice good judgment for a spike on their social media platforms.

Like the ambulance chasing lawyer, the loud voices of the Internet wait for a misstep, a mistake, a faulty theology. Then they chase the story looking for their profits, a growing platform. The Internet creates a distance between the loud voices and those they attack. This, when poorly stewarded, allows us to throw up cheap grace as our license to say what we want, how we want.

When Jesus prayed "on earth as it is in Heaven," did he add "unless you are on the Internet, then by all means have at it"?

Are we the Brilliant Ones when we act this way? Are we the reflections of the new kingdom? Though Christians will not always agree, we can at least act considerately and thoughtfully in our public interaction. The Teacher reminds us, "Whoever belittles his neighbor lacks sense, but a man of understanding remains silent."[11]

Some argue for rebuffing poor theology when it's publicly disseminated. But we must consider the venue and our motives—and the option of silence. We don't always have to be the first to respond, to post, to tweet.

When Christ bids us to follow him, he bids us to die, said Bonhoeffer. Our posture should look like self-sacrifice, not self-love and platform building. Are we fighting the good fight when we seek corrective measures for those with whom we disagree? Or are we just spouting off our opinions?

CONTENT MATTERS

It's not only how we respond but also what we discuss. Toggle forward and Christian infighting and cynicism remain commonplace. We have two close friends, both prominent Christian leaders, who have felt the brunt of the Christian Internet battle mace. They received personal attacks, and one blogger used harsh expletives.

Bright spots do exist, however. Popular blogger and author Tim Challies asked Ann Voskamp for forgiveness because of what he wrote in his review of her book. "I had neglected to remind myself," wrote Challies, "while writing it [the review] that Voskamp is a real person and, not only that, but a sister in Christ. As a writer myself, I ought to remember that words are *meaningful* and revealing and in some way a part of the person who writes them."[12]

In 2011 Tim interviewed Notre Dame professor and church historian Mark Noll. "There's not a whole lot of serious Christian reflection on hot-button issues," said Noll. "Christians are less inclined to offer a well-developed theological position on cultural topics." Noll emphasized the need for Christians to be thoughtful in their handling of serious topics.

In no way are we saying Christians cannot or should not disagree. Healthy dialogue on important topics helps everyone when done well—with discernment and the appropriate motive. When we react before we think *and* pray about the content we disseminate, our light dims.

Let's also not forget our consumption of media. Along with exercising good judgment over what we write, say, and show, we need to evaluate to what and to whom we listen. Developing a voice in the culture does not necessitate adopting the same tone and tactics of the pundits, leaders, and cultural commentators. Mimicking modern media will cast us in their light, which is no light at all. Remember the people walking around with eyes shut tight? From this can only come dark words and dark actions.

"What you say flows from what is in your heart."[13] How fast we forget Jesus' words. We should take up farming or at least a farming perspective. The simple truths from planting and watering and producing fruit warn us: if we feed our roots with poison, our fruit will wither.

"Actions do not emerge from nothing," wrote the late philosopher and spiritual writer Dallas Willard. "They faithfully reveal what is in the heart, and we can know what is in the heart that they depend upon."[14] Willard said we discern each other well—the heart isn't so mysterious. Our words and actions expose our true intent, making it visible for all to see.

The national pop media operates as the theater for the absurd, a stage for reactionary opinions, media stunts, and self-worship. And this is the table at which some evangelicals wish to sit? Christians offer little to the public discussion on searing cultural issues other than ideological hoo-ha from both theologically conservative and liberal perspectives. Has our ambition for influence hobbled our witness?

We need responsible stewards, thinking leaders who reflect on the *why* of what they're writing and speaking about before pushing the "publish" button. Do we as Christians clamor for the Internet's limelight for no other reason than platform building—a dangerous direction, centered on the self rather than others? Christian leaders who hold positions of influence, especially those who lead other

Christians in worship each week, should prayerfully weigh what issues need to be raised and whether those issues will provide "upbuilding"—as Kierkegaard called it—for the family of God.[15]

"The leader of the future," wrote theologian Henri Nouwen, "will be the one who dares to claim his irrelevance in the contemporary world as a divine vocation that allows him or her to enter into a deep solidarity with the anguish underlying the glitter of success and to bring the light of Jesus there."[16]

WHAT WE CAN LEARN FROM BEAUTY AND REFLECTION

Beauty stands in stark contrast to the brute. I (Tim) remember the daffodils, a beauty not astonishing. How they waved to me from a textbook page. How they bobbed in tetrametric dance. My thoughts, of late, have rested on these daffodils as I tried to remember my first encounter with beauty. A beauty I recognized as different, as referent to something other than what I was beholding.

It was in William Wordsworth's poem "I Wandered Lonely as a Cloud" that I encountered an image I would not soon forget:

> A host of golden daffodils,
> Beside the lake, beneath the trees,
> Fluttering and dancing in the breeze.[17]

To this day when I see the spring daffodils I remember this poem; I remember arriving in high school and poetry being the one place I could find beauty.

In his novel *Till We Have Faces*, C. S. Lewis describes the beauty of Psyche (his protagonist) by saying, "It was beauty that did not astonish you till afterwards when you had gone out of sight of her and reflected on it."[18]

I find a resonance with Lewis's description of beauty and Wordsworth's definition of *poetry* as "the spontaneous overflow of powerful feelings: it takes its origin from emotion recollected in tranquillity."[19] Interesting how beauty and poetry find their origins in reflection. How the astonishment was not immediate but expanded and grew as time tooled the image or thought into something transcendent.

A few weeks back I started *The Faerie Queene* by Edmund Spenser, a classic poem of enormous proportions. This poem influenced Lewis's imaginative shaping, and I can see why. Only a few pages in, I stumbled upon a description of a grove of trees that demanded I reread it again and again. Each tree—the oak, the laurel, the pine, and the poplar—was given human-like paint as it drifted beneath the stormy sky, dancing like Wordsworth's daffodils.

The faerie scene of growing tension not only demanded several readings but also invited the whimsy of thought. I fall asleep to these scenes of waving daffodils and the swaying kings of the forest (oaks).

WHAT BEAUTY DEMANDS

Our encounters with beauty turn us to certain realities we cannot neglect. In thinking upon the daffodils I faced knowledge of something else beyond my capacity to explain. It drew desire from me. It resonated with what I understood to be a kind of goodness upon the earth, though I could not and still cannot articulate it.

In all beauty, it seems, we face a healthy bit of morality. This makes sense to me as a Christian because I believe God to be the originator of all things good and true. Beauty resonates in us all and demands not only our attention but also the soulish side of our beings.

Am I hoisting up beauty as a proof for God? Maybe, I wouldn't be the first. But at a more popular level I think what we can learn from beauty (and poetry) is an art form lost in this world of instant publishing, opinions, and hoo-ha. And that art form is *reflection*.

Reflection. Mark Noll commented on it in the interview. It encourages a morality of heart and mind. If we simmer on something long enough, we will find what we did not want to find: our opinions laid waste. Reflection can house the grandest of notions and the deepest of beauties.

But if we surrender our hearts and minds to God, reflection will show us how prideful our pens and thoughts can be—how lazily our opinions are formed. Lewis touches on this idea in his essay "The Seeing Eye." He wrote, "Avoid silence, avoid solitude, avoid any train of thought that leads off the beaten track. Concentrate on money, sex, status, health and (above all) on your own grievances. Keep the radio on. Live in a crowd. Use plenty of sedation. If you must read books, select them very carefully, but you'd be safer to stick to the papers. You'll find the advertisements helpful; especially those with a sexy or snobbish appeal."[20]

In today's world, it pays to be astonishing or provocative. But a holy beauty demands more from us. It demands the rights to our pride and our weak discernment; it demands we wait. It demands we sift through our reactions and realize our point of view can be selfish and wrong.

Let us, as Christians, strive to write pieces of beauty, pieces that demand reflection to produce, pieces that demand our readers reflect as well. So much of what gets passed around in the blogosphere demands little from us.

Provocation and astonishment might garner large followings for a time, but in the long run they wither and are easily deleted.

TRUE CHRISTIAN FREEDOM

How can we join the practice of quiet reflection with true Christian freedom? They seem opposed: restraining from reaction yet exercising freedom. But they are kindred. The apostle Peter reminded his readers: "Live as people who are free, not using your freedom as a cover-up for evil, but living as servants of God. Honor everyone. Love the brotherhood. Fear God. Honor the emperor."[21]

Christian freedom means we are free to follow God's will. We live, like Paul, slaves to the gospel. As such we do not live as permissive agents of cheap grace and license. Rather, we adhere to a specific code: we are to respect every person, we are to love our Christian brothers and sisters, we are to approach God in reverent fear, and we are to show regard for authorities.

It's easy to forget this Christian code. In the pursuit to build leadership platforms, influence, or personal brands and secure a raise or position, we pounce on opportunity. At some level each of us desires to exist and be seen as a person of the inner circle.

GOOSE BUMP BEAUTY

Our friend Ryan O'Neal plays music under the moniker Sleeping at Last. His quiet voice along with the gentle instrumentation of his music screams of beauty. All these whisper-screams live within an industry that produces scores of songs that cast shadows on our world. Ryan's music captures the feeling and emotions of his humanness while pointing to the eternal. Instead of glorifying his brokenness, Ryan acknowledges it as part of life and looks past it to greater themes of love and hope.

According to Ryan, "Beauty is hope; the overwhelming feeling of awe; the cause of goose bumps; light; combination of things that resonate deeply with our souls."[22] Think about how everything felt so big when you were a kid. You saw the world for the first time—a creek was a river, a sapling a mighty oak, a grassy knoll a mountain. The way Ryan described beauty sounds childlike—full of wonder and awe and goose bumps.

Something happens along the path of life, and we lose those childlike eyes. Our vision feels clouded by the shadows. Our exposure to darkness becomes more real. Even worse, at times we revel in those shadows, choosing to hang out within them and ignore the sun around us. Some of us have drifted so far into the shadows that we cannot find our way out. How can we train up children to see the goose bump beauty of this world if we fail to see it? How can we find God if all we do is mill around in the dark?

We cannot escape the shadows. But as Christians we should not be content to live in the shadows. How do we navigate the tension of living in a shadowy world yet not allow those shadows to rule our lives?

Young children rarely see the shadows. They play peekaboo with the light and live in a constant state of discovery and awe. It's no surprise that Jesus said we need the faith of a child to follow him.

We need the wild-eyed wonder of a child to see the beauty. We need the innocence. When we open our eyes again, when we return to a state of discovery like a child, we see that God's brilliance cannot be overcome. No matter how dark our world, no matter how many shadows cast their despair on us, beauty remains.

"Beauty is the remnants of God," said Ryan. It is the "direct result of truth." The bits and pieces of God that slip through the cracks provide the beauty. Even in the shadows we can see glimmers of light. These flickers point to God.

Finding pure darkness is almost impossible. Turn out all the lights on a cold winter night and hold your hand in front of your eyes. You will still see a blurry figure waving back at you. Close your eyes on a sunny day and you still sense light peeking through your lids. Take away all the colors in the rainbow and you won't get darkness; you will get pure and radiant white. No matter how hard you try to black it out, light seeps in through the cracks.

And if that light exists, so does God.

Chapter 3

Brilliance Unseen

SEEING OTHERS AS GOD SEES THEM

Art washes away from the soul the dust of everyday life.
—PABLO PICASSO

There is a crack in everything, that's how the light gets in.
—LEONARD COHEN

[White] is not a mere absence of colour, it is a shining and affirmative thing: as fierce as red, as definite as black. . . . God paints in many colours; but He never paints so gorgeously—I had almost said so gaudily—as when He paints in white.
—G. K. CHESTERTON

Our (Jason's) family finished the Sunday postchurch ritual lunch at the local Mexican dive and paid the check. Hung up at the front door as we grabbed breath mints, we collided with a family— a husband and a wife in their sixties and their grown daughter, all dressed in their Sunday best. The wife looked tidy in a floral print dress, the hemline reaching midcalf, leaving only an inch of flesh-colored hose before the top of her shoes. The husband's short-sleeved yellow shirt matched his diagonal-striped tie in an odd mix of spring colors—green, white, maybe pink, another green, and another yellow. The daughter's dress looked as if it had been cut from the same bolt of fabric as her mother's, and she wore ortho-pedic shoes.

The daughter had a form of mental and physical disability. She smiled at our family as we stood there deciding who would exit next. Then she bent down and whispered a "hello" to our toddler. They mumbled pleasantries, and the girl took my daughter's hand as they danced together in the doorway. The exchange lasted only a minute. Then both families headed to their cars.

We buckled in. My wife's phone rang. She answered. The kids fought over toys. I threw on my sunglasses and retreated into my thoughts. I cried the whole drive home. I couldn't stop.

AN UNSEEN HALLELUJAH

The Wolf River flows northwest, winding its way from Mississippi to Tennessee. In 1960 the river was dammed near its mouth and diverted into the Mississippi River, forming Memphis's Wolf River Harbor. One Thursday night in the spring of 1997, singer-songwriter

Jeff Buckley took a break from rehearsing. Fully clothed he waded into the harbor's water while singing the chorus to "Whole Lotta Love" by Led Zeppelin. Five days later, Buckley's body was found.

Three years before his death, Buckley recorded what many hail as a near perfect rendition of the Leonard Cohen song "Hallelujah." In the recording you can almost touch the tension of conflicting feelings. The song magically comes alive as Buckley's melodic voice gives form and shape and substance to what before were mere words and notes scrawled on a sheet of paper. A writer for *Time* observed that "Buckley treated the 7-min. song like a tiny capsule of human-ity, using his voice to careen between glory and sadness, beauty and pain, mostly just by repeating the word *hallelujah*."[1]

In the song, King David plays a secret chord that pleases the Lord. "The baffled king composing Hallelujah."[2] David's song, Cohen's songwriting, and Buckley's performance are all deemed *pleasing*. Buckley's voice, the structures, the melody, the rules—both applied and broken—all work to make the song *beautiful*.[3]

The singer interpreting the lyrics enhances the song. Then, in this case, something else—the premature death of a rising star—gives "Hallelujah" a haunting quality, moving the composition from pleasing in sound to ethereal in feeling.

Songs, like poetry and prose, possess a beautiful quality, even though we can't always physically see it. Our fingertips can't touch a song. Our eyes don't watch the notes blasting from the horn of an instrument. We can't literally see David playing his lyre. But we *see* it in our imaginations, and we feel it in our beings.

Invisible beauty.

As I drove home from the restaurant, I imagined the hopes

and dreams and excitement the couple probably enjoyed when they first found out they were pregnant. They busied themselves thinking of names: Sally, Mary, Lauren, maybe Anne. Would Anne be a scientist? An artist? A dancer? Maybe the first female president? I imagined them lying in bed at night, staring at the ceiling, Dad with his hand on Mom's belly feeling their Anne kick, laughing about how much they would miss her on her first day of school.

Then I thought about the emotions they felt on the day she was born. What they thought the moment the doctor looked up and said, "Something isn't right."

I thought about how much work goes into taking care of Anne every day and for the past thirty-odd years—dressing her, bathing her, and driving her everywhere.

It's easy to focus on the brokenness and miss the beauty—to get hung up on the what-if of a situation. When you look at Anne, she doesn't dress in the latest trends, and her hair doesn't look like a Hollywood starlet's. No, she's a plain girl in a plain dress with a disability most of us will never understand.

Does the world miss Anne's "Hallelujah"?

A DICHOTOMY OF WORLDS

I found myself, a designer by vocation, looking for something I couldn't see. I live in a world of images, dimension, and proportion. Do the rules I apply in my work to make *something* aesthetically pleasing apply to *everything*, including the human form?

You live in this world too. It's a world of confounding beauty, intricate and simple at the same time. We all enjoy something pleasing to the eye; it can move and convert the heart to new thought, new faith, and new horizons. This is the artist's job.

I love the invisible beauty of Buckley's "Hallelujah," but I also love the beautiful world I wake up to every morning that I see and touch. Where is the line that invisible beauty and physical beauty reconcile with each other?

In the world of design and art, beauty shows up in the form of symmetry and proportion and in the way one object juxtaposes another. These rules that one can follow or break in a certain way make something beautiful—arousing to the eye. Often these objects reflect nature and biology; they mimic the ordered world around us.

Just as a poet uses rhyme and meter as tools to beautify a poem, designers, painters, architects, and others often use the "golden ratio" to do the same in their context. The golden ratio is a mathematical formula that produces aesthetically pleasing proportions. From the Parthenon to the *Mona Lisa*, we can see the golden ratio in most works of great design and art.

Photographers use a tool for composition called "the rule of thirds." This rule frames the photograph in certain ways that draw the eye *through* the image. Applied correctly, this rule can create visual interest, which contributes to the beauty of the photograph.

In a painting, we might look at the use of colors to spot the beauty. The vibrancy of reds, yellows, and blues bounces off the canvas and into the eye. The stark contrast of colors striking a pure balance grips us; the darkness of one color makes the brightness of another pop off the canvas.

Sometimes painters use perspective to show scale and to make a painting look realistic. Other times they use it to distort and skew, offering yet another perspective, one that shows all angles at the same time: past, present, future, top, bottom, side—as Picasso and his cubism do.

In humans, we see beauty too. The golden ratio shows up again, defining proportions of a beautiful face. The more symmetrical a face, the more likely we deem it appealing.

But humans can possess arguably the most arresting beauty on the planet because they possess two parts to their being that work in unison: body and soul. Not only can humans *look* beautiful, but we can also *express* beauty through kind actions, a soft heart, or even a forgiving tone.

Though we live in the physical world, we exist and have our being in an unseen world. And when I looked at Anne, I felt a great disturbance but then a great joy. Anne was a living, breathing juxtaposition of colors, of dark and light, of sound and silence, of brokenness and brilliance. The only difference between us was that she wore most of her brokenness on the outside; inside she shone like the sun.

TRANSFIGURING BEAUTY

Brazen Moses. He asks and he receives. But this is God, Moses.

"Can I see you?" stutters Moses.

"No but yes," replies God. "If you're careful and hide in the cleft of the rock, I will announce myself, and then I will pass by. When I do, you can see my back. I will make all my glory pass before you."

God complies, but he also makes sure Moses tells the people to keep themselves and their animals away from the mountain that he passes over, or they will die. He's just passing, not walking upon it. God tells Moses he has something for him, a new set of tablets. And there, Moses sees his opportunity and he asks.

Moses climbs to the top of the mountain, and God hides him in the cleft of the rock with his hand. Once God passes, he uncovers Moses' face and reveals his back. And then Moses beholds the glory, the goodness, of God. As God passes, he proclaims himself using his personal, intimate name: "The Lord [YHWH], the Lord [YHWH]." And for a moment, Moses sees God.

Back at the foot of the mountain, an Israelite leader greets him: "Moses, you've returned."

"Yes."

"Moses, you're glowing."

"Uh, what?"

"Veil yourself for crying out loud. You look like a sunbeam!"[4]

Today, we don't find many accounts of God appearing before man, showing himself in a literal way. Besides Moses' memorable encounter with God on Mount Sinai, the Bible gives us only one other account of this type of appearance. More than a thousand years after Moses' mountain experience, Jesus is preaching and performing miracles.

After several days of this work, Jesus—along with Peter, James, and John—treks up a mountain to pray. Once settled and praying, the three disciples doze off, a common occurrence for praying disciples.

God appears again on a mountain, in the form of a cloud, but notice what doesn't happen. No one dies. God doesn't instruct anyone to hide or to move animals, and he doesn't require the building of a temple. Why?

Timothy Keller wrote, "Jesus is the temple and tabernacle to end all temples and tabernacles, because he is the sacrifice to end all sacrifices, the ultimate priest to point the way for all priests. . . . [Not] only do the disciples not die, they are surrounded and embraced by the brilliance of God."[5]

FOCUS ON THE BRILLIANCE OF THE GOSPEL

As believers, *we shine as God shines*. We are unlike the unbelievers in this world who live "stone-blind to the dayspring brightness of the Message that shines with Christ, who gives us the best picture of God we'll ever get."[6] Those who believe and follow Christ walk in this brilliant gospel—this handy picture of what God looks like. We just never thought he'd look so odd and invisible and variant.

"God said, 'Light up the darkness!' and our lives filled up with light as we saw and understood God in the face of Christ, all bright and beautiful."[7] To shine as he shines means that our minds and hearts emerge from the darkness, our imaginations baptized in the light of the gospel. But you and I know that real life doesn't shimmer with magic dust. We want so much to bask in God's light, but how? At times he seems so far away from our daily lives.

If we can see God, why do we feel blind; the weight of the day-to-day drudgery of life; the suffering, guilt, and brokenness crushing our sight and obscuring our vision of his glory? These feelings make God seem far from us. They dim our brightness and keep our eyes covered. They force us into a life lived from the shadows.

When God feels far away, the temptation to clutch man's glory grows. We cast our golden images just as the dancing Israelites did while waiting for Moses, wondering whether God would ever give them their promised land. Our popular culture focuses on humans' glory where our accomplishments and our treasures accumulate to the praise of other people. In the shadows our vision falters to the point we think our accomplishments and treasures will last forever.

During the height of the Roman Empire, the generals paraded through the streets of Rome in their chariots to celebrate a victorious battle. Caesar allowed a procession after a victory, but he demanded that a slave stand next to the general and whisper in his ear, *"Sic transit gloria mundi,"* which translates "so passes away the glory of the world."[8] It was a reminder to the general that all glory fades.

Deep down, we recognize that man's glory dissipates. God's glory, however, never fades. He abides. His brilliance covers us forever and ever, always.

We don't experience the same things as Moses or the disciples, but we do have experiences. The New Testament says that we become temples of God when we invite Christ into our lives. He lives within us just as he did in the Holy of Holies. Whatever was so powerful and holy, whatever was so intense that man couldn't view it and animals couldn't touch the mountain when it passed over, whatever was so strong that it bleached clothes and made faces to shine so brightly they needed a veil, that thing, that spirit and being, is inside us. We carry it. The temple shroud split, and now each of us is a temple. God is in us, and he is all around us.

We won't see God face-to-face until we meet him in the new kingdom, but we see his radiance everywhere. When we can poke our heads out of the shadows, we can spot the uncovered passing of

God's glory. We can see his truth, his goodness, and his beauty, and not only can we see the brilliance, but we carry it with us.

BACK AT THE RESTAURANT

As I thought about Anne on my drive home, my eyes shifted past her outward appearance. I saw her from a new perspective, a perspective that was fuller than the doorway encounter and more like cubism. I saw the prebirth joy and postbirth cascade of emotions. I saw the unabashed playfulness of Anne dancing in the doorway. I saw sorrow and hope and love, and I saw all of it at the same time.

To God, Anne isn't a girl wearing clunky shoes who struggles with a disability. No, God sees Anne as a living temple where beauty resides and its sparkling dust collects on her soul. His thumbprint presses into her being, his image wrapped up in hers.

As a Christian, when I look at Anne—when I look at people, when I look at myself—this is what I should see. When I first saw Anne, I saw the brutish nature of our fallen world, her twisted and decaying body. But when I saw her as God sees her, in her cubist form, I saw beauty contrasted with the broken, and the contrast made her beauty more brilliant.

Chapter 4

A Rocket Ship to God

WE CAN'T SEE GOD THROUGH THE CLOUDED EYES OF CYNICISM

---

*For centuries now our culture has cultivated the idea that the
skeptical person is always smarter than one who believes. You can
be almost as stupid as a cabbage as long as you doubt.*
—DALLAS WILLARD, *HEARING GOD*

*The thing is: The cynics, they can only speak of the dark, of the obvious,
and this is not hard. For all its supposed sophistication, it's cynicism that's
simplistic. In a fallen world, how profound is it to see the cracks?*
—ANN VOSKAMP

*When God wants to carry a point with his children,
he plants his argument into the instincts.*
—RALPH WALDO EMERSON

A passageway exists that leads to a world of treasure. Secret passages are always welcome, especially when you're in a bind, when life slants unfair, or when you become lost in life's shadows.

You see, we are forever searching for the beautiful in this life—things or people or places that make us feel like kids again. They possess the ability to retwist what the world bends and distorts into what we always thought things ought to be. They possess an innocence procured from the infinite.

Innocence, it seems, is the skeleton key to beauty. And the door leading into beauty does not open easily. We must turn the key and push through, gripping the key of innocence all the while. Once through the door we must reacquaint ourselves with this mysterious passageway—our holy imaginations. And then we must continue into the secret hall until we come up through the trapdoor into the sun.

There, we find this new and glittery world of treasure. It looks strangely familiar, like a memory from one of our childhood books. And once we are there, in this world of treasure, the shadows dissipate. There, innocence is reborn. There, beauty flourishes the way it did in our dreams, the way we always thought it should.

How does this new world of innocence and beauty change us?

We find new vision as we view our surroundings through the kaleidoscope lens of belief. "Fortunate is the person who sees with eyes and heart together," wrote Jewish theologian Abraham Heschel.[1] We see the world for what it is, a brutalized mess. And yet we are not dismayed. Rather, we breathe deeply and set out on a rescue mission; we "hate it enough to change it, and yet love it enough to think it worth changing."[2]

When we find our innocence, we find beauty afresh. It rests in the hand of God—a hand that holds us high above this world's afflictions, high enough to see the light behind the sun.

MORNING DANCES AND ROCKET SHIPS

I (Tim) am the father of three girls—Lyric, Brielle, and Zion. Daily they invite me to crawl inside and poke around the beauty of their innocence, their breath-haze on the glass of my life.

Allow me to take you back a few years. Two exhausted parents: one nursing our first little girl—a spirited one-year-old—the other plowing through graduate school on the side. On this particular morning, Lyric was lying in bed with us. It was early and blue, the night's veil already lifting.

In my ear I hear her skin burrow into mine. It sounds like nuzzling. Her cheek presses in, then a small blue eyeball emerges and squints a smile. I hear a muffled giggle. I kiss the squinting eye and seize the everlasting moment, locking it away in my memory.

"Da-da, Da-da, Da-da." Lyric can already speak to me, if only on a visceral level. Maybe we're speaking some ancient love language that joins our souls. Maybe I just need coffee.

Groggy giggle, giggle, giggle. The morning light highlights her strawberry hair as it blurs back down into the pillows and then burrows into my embrace.

What begins in the waking bed with father and little one moves to the closet. We pick out her outfit together: purple flowery dress, then hat, then jeans under the dress. Now belly laughs ensue with a "catch me if you can" that ends with her arms wrapped around my neck. We head downstairs to start breakfast.

By now the sun blasts full throttle, shooting through the kitchen windows and bouncing off Lyric's smiling blue eyes. In her red knit hat, she parades through the kitchen, calling my name and waving her hands. It's our own ballroom, and we play-dance in step: me from her, me to her, me holding her.

I hit "play" on the stereo. She nods approval to the new song, and we dance some more. The music rises vibrant and loud—the way she likes it. I pull her close, humming the tune in her ear. She draws close to hear more. And in delight, she rests her head on my chest as I dance her around the kitchen.

Dough bubbles out of the waffle iron while the press steams with coffee. The music lifts with the sunlight as we dance in and out of its beams—from shadow to shaft, trying to stay within the beams. Finally we rest, standing together in the light. It colors us as she colors me with her giggling and nuzzling.

The giggly mornings pass. The belly laughs and dances pile up. Lyric is four now. We sit in her bed and look at her "God book." It's a children's Bible filled with paintings and vignettes that show the narrative of God's love for humans. She flips to the last third of the book and shows me the page containing the three crosses. And then the conversation begins.

"Daddy, can we go see God?"

"Would you like to?"

"Yes. We can take my rocket ship."

"You have a rocket ship?"

"Of course, Daddy. Don't worry. I know how to drive it. You taught me."

"I did?" I don't remember that part.

"You have to get buckled in. Now sit back and close your eyes, Daddy."

She's holding an imaginary steering wheel. I peek and see her squinting hard and smiling just as hard. I close my eyes once more.

"Blast off!" she yells.

Her abrupt shout startles me.

"Up, up, up. High we go, past the clouds. Up, up, up we go, past the sun." Her voice rises to a squeal.

"Up, up, up, past the moon, past the stars. Uh-oh! We have to get past the Ampershavers!"

"The who?"

"The Ampershavers. They're really dangerous. Close your eyes. Here we go!"

She tenses up, and our imaginary rocket ship banks to the left, then to the right. She finally relaxes her shoulders and breathes a dramatic sigh of relief.

"Whew! That was close. So here we are."

"Is it safe to get out?" I ask.

"Sure. Sure, it's safe."

"Look, there's God's house over there." I'm getting into the charade.

"Yes, yes. Let's go. Do you think he will mind if we go in, Daddy?"

"I don't think he'll mind. Do you want to talk to him?"

"I do. Oh, look! There he is."

She points past me and I turn. And there he is, sitting at a gargantuan oak table that shows the wear of eternity. He hasn't shaved in a while. I wonder if he's aware of the earthly stereotypes. I wasn't expecting him to be so massive. He's less like Gandalf and more like Ariel's father in *The Little Mermaid*. What can I say? With three daughters my life is one big Disney princess movie.

Lyric starts into a litany of questions, walking him through the crucifixion of Jesus in her God book—she brought it with her. At one point she stops asking questions and starts talking about how God died so the bad things would be forgotten. God doesn't talk much. He listens. Finally Lyric finishes her God inquiry and leads me out of his house back to the rocket ship.

"Well, it's time to go home, Daddy."

"Yeah? Well, I am getting tired."

"Me too."

The flight back is quick, though we barely make it past the Ampershavers. We land under a fleece blanket where I buckle her into sleep. She falls to sleep heavily as I ease out of the bed.

"Good night, Lyric. I love you," I whisper as I close the door.

CALLING THE LAPSED SOUL

When Lyric retold the story of Jesus' death to God, she didn't differentiate the Son from the Father. She turned the pages of her God book and said to him, "And here *you* are in front of the mean people. And then *you* died on this cross, and they put *you* behind this rock."

In her intimate divine discussion she accomplished what I so often fail to do in my spiritual life. She reached out to God by reaching through his Son.

"How will we know the way?" asked Thomas the disciple.

"I AM the Way," replied Jesus. Don't you get it? When you see me you've seen the Father. If you want to know *the way* to God, then follow me!"

Poor Thomas. If only he could have seen through Lyric's eyes.

If only I could as well. Innocence allows us to see God aright—to see him how we were meant to see him. We are able to see him because we are able to talk to Jesus in a way free from the guilt and shame with which the world tries to paint us. As children we skip, we pretend, and we read books, all in the fullness of God's pleasure. As adults we experience the pressures of success, acceptance, and doing the right thing robbing us of simple pleasures, but pleasures that nonetheless help us establish our confidence and trust in God. The simple pleasures in this life, the ones we experience as children but too often forget about as adults, give us a sense of home. C. S. Lewis said, "The deepest likings and impulses of any man are the raw material, the starting-point" God has given to us.[3]

That evening it was as if Lyric was transported to Eden, that original paradise of unabated relational intimacy with Yahweh. The place of *ought*—the intended and perfect glory of man. Lyric was at peace in the presence of the One who walked in the garden with Adam and Eve, moving through like the presence of a hurricane. She was at peace because she was *innocent*. She hadn't been expelled from the garden yet. The world hadn't sunk its talons into her. The brutishness of fallen man hadn't claimed her on the altar of sensuality. Her sin nature hadn't grown to full capacity yet. She lived in the grand in-between. She knew enough to tell Daddy, "No!" but not enough to be blinded by pride and pain and disappointment. She was safe for a brief time. She saw God and his Son and was not ashamed.

She talked to God on the rocket ship trip with the same free-dom that allows her to run naked in the backyard. She did not need to be told *the way* like Thomas, like me. She *lived* in it.

When we're young, we live within God's glory for a time. When we grow older and become sophisticated adults, we listen to our sons and daughters talk about rocket ships and Ampershavers, and we marvel at the sheer simplicity of mind. We're dazzled by the utter beauty of the moment, of the child, of the innocence.

We think of our childhoods and say, "If only." That time of life fades now like the Polaroids from yesteryear. We talk of those beau-tiful times of innocence with nostalgia, basking in the memory. But that's it, isn't it? Just memory.

Those nostalgic thoughts create a longing within us. But we're too smart to really believe we could return to such a time, even though the longing feels true, as if that's where we're supposed to be.

At some point, however, we recognize our nakedness, and shame enters the picture. We push the longing and all the nostal-gia down, locking it into a memory chest. We realize now that the grand in-between has dissipated, and innocence, as we like to say, is lost. In the twenty-first century innocence might as well be a relic from antiquity, for the cynicism has eaten up innocence.

FROM INNOCENCE TO THE SOILED SELF

One of my professors in graduate school walked our class through an insightful time line of the great modern thinkers that showed the decline from belief into cynicism. He began with Descartes. The famous rationalist remains known for his "I think, therefore I am."

Then David Hume said no, it's not only that we think; it's what we experience. The empiricist, skeptical of Descartes's idea, said we can know only because of what we can see and touch.

Immanuel Kant took a hard left and responded with the notion that what we see and touch and experience is mere perception and each person possesses a different perception. Kant's notion gave way to Nietzsche's nihilism—life is meaningless.

Modern thought reached out in an attempt to know and became skeptical of reality and truth. That skepticism eventually gave way to cynicism, and cynicism has given us little hope of returning to Eden—or anything of the sort. We might call modern thought's decline "a slide from innocence to the soiled self."

The romantic poet William Blake prophesied as much in his epic *Songs of Innocence and of Experience* (1789–94). *Songs of Innocence* came first. It is a collection of poems and engravings symbolizing one side of the human condition. Some think this work represents his state before he was soiled by the worldliness that accompanies the frivolities of the adult life—parties, gossip, dissipation, and so on. In his expression of innocence Blake shows us the tie between Jesus, the Lamb, and each of us as children, for Christ himself *became* a child and then died as an innocent lamb:

> Little Lamb, I'll tell thee,
> Little Lamb, I'll tell thee:
> He is called by thy name,
> For he calls himself a Lamb.
> He is meek, & he is mild;
> He became a little child.

I a child, & thou a lamb,

We are called by his name.[4]

Songs of Experience, on the other hand, describes the soiled state of the human condition, what we call in this book "the shadows of life." Blake saw humankind—Descartes, Hume, and Kant— embrace reason and abandon imagination. He called out to the "lapsed Soul" in the introduction to his experience poems.[5] In the poems the earth responds to Blake's call by saying that she's held captive by Reason and held down by materialism. The tension of innocence and experience, however, somehow seems dominated by the experience, the brutality of life crushing the beauty of inno- cence and abandoning it.

If our cynical world says we can never return to a state of child- likeness, if it says this life begins in innocence but ends in meaningless existence punctuated by death, then Jesus' words to Nicodemus in John's gospel account are exactly what you and I and the people of this age need to hear: "I tell you the truth, unless you are born again, you cannot see the Kingdom of God."[6]

Jesus accomplished something stunning when he gave himself up to the tree. He carved a way back into our mothers' wombs—not literally, of course, but spiritually. And through this rebirth, we find the power to enter once again into that innocent place of God's glory. But the pathway into life is not easy.

FROM BIRTH INTO BELIEF

Nature shows us how the earth must sleep in wintry death before new life can spring forth once again. And that birthing process is marked by pain.

The pangs of birth are everywhere. The earth erupts, and the dirt pushes back to reveal the glory green of new plant life reaching to the sun. The flowers emerge from the ground and bloom. Pollen covers the landscape like a yellow blanket, and every so often the dark clouds gather and rise high into the heavens. They unleash their torrents, unannounced. The thunder quakes, the earth shudders, and the willows and oaks tremble beneath the dark rains.

Have you ever waited on the front porch while a storm approaches? I have. The thunder rolls out and proclaims the coming of the wind like a royal crier preparing the commoners for the magnificence of the king.

Who doesn't stare at a heaving storm? Who is not caught in the overwhelming sensation of nature holding its breath for the torrents, lightning, and hail?

The innocence of new life quickens amid the tumult of the changing season, and in this time of life awakening we learn how storms invigorate new life. When the winds pass and the boughs ease, the tendrils climb and the buds open. Beauty waits in every blossom, in every field, in every drop of rain shining on the grass.

All new life rages forth—nature's *and* ours. I remember when my brother's first son was born. I see that new little life in a frame on my shelf now. Loving arms, tender and able, hold him as he suckles the milk that grows him. My brother named him Judah, a lion cub wrapped in the skin of an infant boy. In this picture he's only a few months old, but already his life has impressed so many. His presence is like the thunder echoing in the valleys, ringing in the canyons.

We live in a world where innocence and pain can coexist. God made it so. The storm brings unruly power, even devastation. And yet with the storms of spring come the rains that give life. "When a woman gives birth, she has a hard time," wrote John the Beloved, "there's no getting around it. But when the baby is born, there is joy in the birth. This new life in the world wipes out memory of the pain."[7]

When the Lamb came to live among us, meek and mild, he showed us how even in pain and the tumult of life, innocence will spring forth yet again.

It is the pain that draws us to new life. It is the victory over death that we love to see, smell, taste, and hear. "Aha, you Death! Again life springs from the womb of our beloved! Again, you wither in the shadows shriveling in the throes of glory-birth!"

Into what, though, will little Judah and my Lyric enter? They will encounter that first moment when they realize their nakedness. They will fail. They will fall. They will hurt. They will betray and be betrayed. But their lives will not exist in any kind of garden that values the holy virtue of their existence.

They will encounter the unnatural and twisted: people and forces seeking only to destroy. Never before in human history has life itself fallen under so heavy a fist. Abortion, child abandonment (orphan crisis), pedophilia, sex trafficking, hypersexualization of children, and child slavery show the world to be not only unsafe for the innocent but diabolically so. Children leave their innocence behind early on in this world.

What is to keep them from becoming cynical? What will incite hope in them? And what about you and me? Have we fallen into the way of the cynic? Is the beauty of innocence mere nostalgia?

56

A LIVING BELIEF

We should look to belief in God as our gateway into innocence. But it isn't enough to believe. After all, the demons believe and shudder. We are more than demons. The people who ushered Jesus into Jerusalem by shouting, "Hosanna!" were the same ones who, within a week, were shouting, "Crucify him!" They *believed* at first. They believed when they saw the signs and wonders. They believed when they saw Jesus raise Lazarus from the dead. They believed in a Messiah who fit their expectations, who fit their profile, who fit their desires: someone to save them from Roman oppression.

But their belief ended when Jesus fell into the custody of the Sanhedrin. Where does our belief begin and where does it end, as if it should ever end? The writer of Hebrews said, "The fundamental fact of existence is that this trust in God, this faith, is the firm foundation under everything that makes life worth living. It's our handle on what we can't see. The act of faith is what distinguished our ancestors, set them above the crowd."[8]

If our faith is a handle on what we can't see, many of us are limping through life with a broken handle. We say we believe; we grant our intellectual assent to the idea of God and his one-of-a-kind Son. But our lifestyles say something else. We keep crazy work schedules so we won't be left in want. In doing so we have forgotten the sparrow and the lily—they neither toil nor want. Then we wonder why we're burned out and stressed and so negative all the time, and we wonder why church feels so empty.

We've forgotten what it means to be children of God. We've wandered away from the innocence that comes in truly believing and living as if it is so. And maybe we never *really* wanted to follow him in the first place. Maybe some of us aren't Christians at all, just religious.

I believe if we set out to follow Christ, we will find ourselves in a state of innocence, where the magic of our redemption returns us to a place where we see things more clearly.[9] When we become born again, our lives should change. Our perspective should change. And yet even though we should experience wholesale change, I also believe as Christians we can fall into ditches along our spiritual pathways that, if we're not careful, can render our belief mute. I spent several years in such a ditch. I'm sure many of us have.

But God does not intend life with him to lead us into a ditch. We chose the ditch when we wandered into the world of shadows. He has so much to show us, but our belief fails us. Like the Israelites who wanted to cover all their bases, they wanted God but also wanted to appease the pagan gods of land and rain so their crops would grow. Sometimes we try to cover all our bases: great paying job, nice house, safe neighborhood, good church, money in the bank, comprehensive insurance. Those things are not bad in and of themselves, but they can become our pagan gods—our backup plan in case this God we can't see doesn't come through for us.

How weak! How so very old of us, as Chesterton would say. We are not children but dry old bones wasting away in a lonely valley.[10] We've forgotten God gave us our imaginations so that we could look into the invisible and *see* him, so that we could *know* that faith in him will keep us.

And although the storms of life may come, we waver not. For we *know* that he will calm the storm. He has done so before. When the barrenness of winter comes into our lives through death and loss and betrayal, cynicism is kept at bay because we *know* that new life *will* come and *has* come through Jesus. We see the wonder of God's glory through the kaleidoscope lens of belief. "If you're serious about living this new resurrection life with Christ, act like it," wrote the apostle Paul. "Pursue the things over which Christ presides. Don't shuffle along, eyes to the ground, absorbed with the things right in front of you. Look up, and be alert to what is going on around Christ—that's where the action is. See things from his perspective."[11]

My heart pounds even as I type this chapter because I'm not just thinking about belief; I'm living in it. During the last few months my wife, Chris, and I have been making plans to move our three girls with us to England. We sense a call to move so that I can pursue a PhD at King's College, London. It's the scariest thing we've ever done together. It's one thing to live on a little bit of money and food when you're newlyweds. It's quite another to have three daughters who look to you for everything, and you decide to up and move to a new continent. Some nights I curl up in my study and just whisper to God like my girls whisper to me when I tuck them in. We can plan and prepare all we want, but in the end it comes down to belief: *God will provide; he said so.*

"He stood there," wrote Kierkegaard about Abraham in his wonderful little book *Fear and Trembling*, "the old man with his only hope! But he did not doubt, he did not look in anguish to left or right, he did not challenge heaven with his prayers. He knew it was God the Almighty that tried him, he knew it was the hardest sacrifice that could be demanded of him; but he also knew that no sacrifice was too hard when God demanded it—and he drew the knife."[12]

Believing in the unseen keeps us childlike and, in a sense, returns us to a kind of innocence. When I was twenty and twenty-five and even thirty, I struggled to make sense of God and my relationship with Jesus. At times it all seemed so muddled. My faith, however, clarifies the more I age. The clarity I gain from growing with Christ and trusting in him—for everything from housing to income to the health of my daughters—returns me to a familiar place. I find myself caught under the stars like a child, wondering about God. But not just wondering, worshiping and talking out loud to him.

The older I get in my faith, the simpler and more innocent I become. I'm not boasting of my innocence here. Rather, I'm reveling in and praising God's work of shaping me, of his desires becoming my own. I can almost feel this happening daily in simple decisions and tastes. Television shows and movies I used to watch I find pale and flavorless. I find myself looking for a kind of beauty the world cannot deliver—yes, I do find remnants of this beauty in the world but not the true essence of it. I find *that* when I find Jesus in the quiet of the morning.

The atheist Richard Dawkins said belief in God is just like believing in the tooth fairy or Santa Claus. We should abandon our belief in God just like we abandon our belief in jolly old Saint Nick. To a person like Dawkins, we come of age when we move from belief to "evidence-based thinking."[13] Dawkins is right. Most everyone abandons belief in Santa Claus by age five.

But what about people who find Christ through experiences at Harvard or through tragedy later in life or through a friend at work? Have they stumbled on a kind of Santa Claus later in life, a kind of fairy-tale prince who satisfies all their earthly longings? Or have they stumbled upon something more profound, something that provides the innocence we experience when we find glimpses of pure beauty? The beautiful thing about the Christian faith is that it is not only rational but also relational and experiential. And as we grow in our relationship with God, we don't find him to be a figment of our imaginations. Rather, we find that he orchestrates our imaginations, that he loves us and cares for us, and in the relationship our affections for him grow.

If you want the ability to board a rocket ship to God, *believe* and *act* as if who you believe in is real. If you want to crawl into the spiritual womb again, do so. But be prepared for the storms it will take to get you through the birth canal.

You must then live on the earth while staring into heaven. But that's not so hard. Just don't forget about the Ampershavers—they're pretty dangerous. And when you make it past them, you'll see that what you've been staring into all this time wasn't only heaven but heaven's joy—Jesus himself. There he is, sitting at his gargantuan oak table. Go ahead. Ask him something. And become a child again.

Chapter 5

Mist Kiss

FIGHTING TO STAY SURRENDERED TO GOD

I hesitate now, as I did then, at the attempt to give my vision utterance. Never were words so beggared for an abridged translation of any Scripture of Nature.
—FITZ HUGH LUDLOW, SPEAKING OF YOSEMITE

Reading about nature is fine, but if a person walks in the woods and listens carefully, he can learn more than what is in books, for they speak with the voice of God.
—GEORGE WASHINGTON CARVER

Thousands of tired, nerve-shaken, over-civilized people are beginning to find out that going to the mountains is going home; that wildness is a necessity . . . as fountains of life.
—JOHN MUIR

My (Jason's) three-year-old baby girl perched herself in the Kelty high on my back. Her hands tapped the top of my head, an offbeat metronome that kept the time to her made-up song. "Baby bear, baby bear, baby bear," she sang again and again as we hiked. Nana mentioned that we might see a mamma and her cubs. The anticipation mounted as our family navigated the park. We all started to believe that a baby bear might appear at the next bend.

The boys navigated the trail at their own hyperpace. Always a "Hey, slow down!" away from the rest of us, they jumped from boulder to rock to tree to boulder. Each section of the path unveiled a new adventure, a new danger, a new challenge, a new discovery.

"Whoa! Look over here," yelled one.

"What's this plant, Dad?" asked the other. "Is it poisonous?"

"I'm like Bear Grylls. I can climb up this rock, then straddle down the crack."

"Look at me. I can do it too. Except I go backward."

Five days earlier we had entered Yosemite National Park on California Route 140, through the Big Oak Flat entrance, and snaked our way through the mountains that lead to the valley floor. Each turn in the road uncovered a new view of the surrounding mountains and the meadows below, each vista more majestic and grand than the one before. The whole drive felt like a tease, as if God was our tour guide, running in front of us, pointing and yelling over his shoulder, "Oh yeah, you think that is amazing? Well, wait until you drive around the bend and see what I did over there."

As CA-140 unwinds itself you start to catch glimpses of the largest granite monolith in the world, El Capitan. The mighty rock sits stoic, a Stonewall Jackson sort of character posing for his portrait after a hard-fought battle. Off to the east a massive mountain hook stretches four thousand feet above the ground, snagging the passing clouds. Together, the two formations stand on either side of the valley floor, keeping guard over the wildflowers that sprinkle the meadow.

In 1851 a group of California state militiamen worked their way into the valley; they were among the first white men to enter the area and record what they saw. Lafayette Bunnell, a young doctor on the expedition, attempted to describe his feelings upon entering the area. "As I looked, a peculiar exalted sensation seemed to fill my whole being, and I found my eyes in tears with emotion," wrote Bunnell. "I have here seen the power and glory of a Supreme being: the majesty of His handy-work is in that 'Testimony of the Rocks.'"[1]

If you think you know something about God, visit Yosemite and then think again. Whatever vision of majesty or beauty or creativity you might have shatters in the backdrop of the reverence of one of the most spectacular places on the planet. Walking the trails of Yosemite feels like walking toward heaven, as if behind the granite door of El Capitan and Half Dome sits the Great City. With each step in the park you feel farther from the world and closer to God.

"Walk away quietly in any direction and taste the freedom of the mountaineer," noted nature's apostle John Muir, a self-described unknown nobody. "Camp out among the grasses and gentians of glacial meadows, in craggy garden nooks full of Nature's darlings. Climb the mountains and get their good tidings, Nature's peace will flow into you as sunshine flows into trees . . . while cares will drop off like autumn leaves."[2]

Muir realized we can lose sight of who we are, but the wild gives us a way to rediscover ourselves. Standing alone in the Godscape, Muir believed that we slow down enough to let our thoughts catch up to us.

"Baby bear, baby bear, baby bear," her made-up song continued as we snaked up the trail to Vernal Fall, a 317-foot waterfall that flows off the Merced River. During the hike, I turned from a man trying to keep his kids from falling into the ravine into a child looking for a baby bear. I, too, started to anticipate something, anything.

At our final stop on the trail, a wooden bridge crossed a section of the waterfall. The boys crossed over to chase squirrels. Mom took baby girl for a snack, and I took the Kelty off to rest my aching back. As I stood alone on the bridge wondering at the mountainscape, it was hard not to feel like a tiny speck of nothingness on a microcosm of an infinitely undiscoverable universe.

There, on that bridge, with water pounding the rocks below, I couldn't escape the feeling that I was an *unknown nobody*.

NOTHING BUT NOTHING

"Simplicity, simplicity, simplicity!" exclaimed Henry David Thoreau.[3] He lived by the rule of carrying "as little as possible."[4] Thoreau, along with Muir, chose to live a life rooted in simplicity. They possessed enough to get by, stripping themselves of the distractions brought on by modern life. In a world inundated with stuff, simplicity seems more and more like a good idea.

Yosemite carries its own form of simplicity. Not in the grandeur of its design but in the way it strips out the day to day of life. A pair of hiking shoes, a pack, some water, and that's about all you need to enjoy the park. In this reductionist mode, your mind clears; no cell phone buzzing in your pocket, no laptop dinging you with e-mails.

In Yosemite, you see towering oaks, cascading waterfalls, and giant monoliths. You're surrounded by some of the largest natural creations, most complex organisms, and most delicate ecosystems in the world. Yet in all that you feel the simplicity of life. Yosemite acts as a contradiction in that you could have everything yet nothing at the same time.

The idea of simplicity resonates in the design world. We see it in products by Apple that "just work" with a single button or in the sleek lines of an architect like Renzo Piano or in the use of simple materials in the furniture of Charles and Ray Eames. Japanese designer Kenya Hara advocates for something beyond simple; he preaches the idea of emptiness. He uses the example of a Japanese steak knife versus a Western steak knife. A well-designed Western steak knife maintains simplicity in its form with nothing but a blade and a handle, sculpted to match the hand of the user. The ergonomic nature of the handle signals to the cook exactly where to place the thumb and hand and, in essence, shows the cook how to use the knife.

In contrast, the handle on a traditional Japanese steak knife extends with nothing to indicate where the thumb or fingers should sit. Instead, the wooden cylinder obeys the chef's preference. The chef can handle the knife any way she wants, allowing her skill to dictate the best way to hold and use the instrument. Both knives boast simple and superb designs, but only the Japanese knife maintains emptiness.

"Emptiness," explains Hara, "holds the possibility of being filled."[5]

Hara's idea of emptiness suggests life is full of possibilities, full of value. Nothing is truly empty. Instead, everything is waiting to be used and fulfilled. When my daughter rounded the bend on the trail, she saw the possibility of the bear. There are no inputs in her life to suggest otherwise. Why wouldn't there be a bear? I don't count this as silly childhood naïveté; instead it is the wonderful emptiness of her mind.

Maybe that's why Muir dedicated his life to Yosemite. He found more than the filtering of life's distractions; he found the vast emptiness of the place. He saw something at which to wonder, a land full of potential and discovery. In my own way, I found the same, moments of God-wonder and self-discovery.

I need those moments of reflection. The simplicity of the time leads me to quiet reflection. My mind empties. My tired self empties. And through the emptying process a rediscovery starts and finds possibility.

Finding emptiness seems difficult for us as adults. Life experiences, society, and multiple contexts and inputs work to fill us—the hurtful home life, the bully at school, the lost job, the marriage that can't seem to find its sea legs. Or maybe our lives are full of nothing but success, and pride pours in, filling us. In both, our perspective conforms and possibility outside our current situation diminishes.

THE END AND THE BEGINNING

"It's time," said Heather, jarring me out of my early morning mind sludge.

I sprang up, ran around our room, then the house, gathering our things. As I backed the car down the driveway, the talk radio blared the news: a plane crashed into a tower of the World Trade Center.

As we drove into downtown Atlanta, it became apparent this wasn't a freak air-travel accident. It was a nation-changing historic event. We listened to the radio in stunned silence as a Wellesian account of the morning unfolded. No commentator knew exactly what was happening, but they all agreed it was bad. When we walked into the lobby of the hospital, everyone stood watching the television as the first tower crumbled.

September 11, 2001. That's all you need to say, and everyone understands. It marked a period of time in America's history, and it marked a period of time for our family. At 4:28 p.m. on that day, our first son entered the world.

The nation heaved in chaos, yet this beautiful little boy slept in our arms. As we questioned the *why* of the attack, others wrote to tell us how the birth of our son gave them hope. To them, his birth meant the world kept turning, things would be okay, and innocence still existed amid the terror. He was only a day old, and God was already using him.

Two days after his birth, my phone rang. It was my boss. He walked me through the situation at work. Cutbacks and layoffs loomed. The company didn't need me anymore.

And that was that. No job, no insurance, no income, and no savings.

Sometimes I think God moves and pulls us into the places he wants us with care and tenderness. It can almost feel like a happy accident. Other times I think he gives us a swift kick. Losing my job was the swift kick.

The experience caused a forced emptying. The pride I felt from having a good job that paid well left. The illusion of control over my life disappeared. All the answers I thought I knew turned to questions as I wondered what a man, a husband, a father looked like.

Hara used the example of a bowl: "A creative mind, in short, does not see an empty bowl as valueless, but perceives it as existing in a transitional state, waiting for the content that will eventually fill it; and this creative perspective instills power in the emptiness."[6]

The gospel shows us we have hope for what is to come, not just what is. When I saw the world like a grown-up who needed to make money or to just get through the day, I filled myself with past tendencies of control or pride. But when God emptied me, he opened my eyes, and I saw things with the wonder of a child, full of possibility. And then God's work began.

Until that time I lived as the ergonomic handle of a Western knife, placing God's hand in comfortable positions on my life, telling him how he could best use me. When I lost my job, my handle changed to the smooth wooden cylinder of the Japanese knife, and God said, "This is better. I want to use you this way."

BACK ON THE BRIDGE

As I stood on the bridge I thought, *God, in all this, how do you remember me? How do you manage to take care of and love and keep tight hold of something as insignificant as me?*

As the thought bounced around, the water below crashed against a rock, and a mist brushed against my face. For a second, the cool mist felt as if God bent down and kissed me on the cheek. He heard my thoughts and with a mist replied, "I know you are there. I see you and I hear you and I love you. I am with you always. I take care of the birds, son. Are you not greater than they are? Jason, I love you. You are my child. I adopted you into my family. You are my heir. A king and a priest over all that you see."

I wonder if seeing the brilliance means unseeing ourselves. Or seeing our true selves through God's eyes—delighting in who we are, what we do, how we do it. We marvel at the world around us and discover our place in it. We empty ourselves of cynicism, self-doubt, loathing, shame, pride, and all the rest. And when we do, God fills us with possibility, and we find him standing with us ready to splash water on our tired faces.

Chapter 6

An Ostrich, a Mystery, and the Wail of Contentment

HOW CONTENTMENT AND THANKFULNESS HELP US
DEFEAT AFFLICTION AND FIND PEACE WITH GOD

Afflictions . . . make the heart more deep, more experimental, more knowing
and profound, and so, more able to hold, to contain, and bear more.
—JOHN BUNYAN

There is nothing that can replace the absence of someone dear to us, and one
should not even attempt to do so; one must simply persevere and endure it. At first
that sounds very hard, but at the same time it is a great comfort, for one remains
connected to the other person through the emptiness to the extent it truly remains
unfilled. It is wrong to say that God fills the emptiness; God in no way fills it but
rather keeps it empty and thus helps us preserve—even if in pain—our authentic
communion. Further, the more beautiful and full the memories, the more difficult
the separation. But gratitude transforms the torment of memory into silent joy. One
bears what was lovely in the past not as a thorn but as a precious gift deep within.
—DIETRICH BONHOEFFER, *LETTERS AND PAPERS FROM PRISON*

Contentment can only happen as we increase desire, let it run itself
out toward its fulfillment, and carry us along with it.
—BRENT CURTIS AND JOHN ELDREDGE, *THE SACRED ROMANCE*

In 2012, I (Tim) helped former NFL MVP Randall Cunningham write a book titled *Lay It Down*. It tells the tragic story of his youngest son's passing when he was two and a half. Randall had returned from a trip to California. It was a typical day in Las Vegas, the city where he pastors a church, coaches a local track team, and grows his family. As he drove down the avenue toward his house, he noticed an ambulance, some police cars, and a coroner's truck.

Something was off.

Randall told me he *knew* something had happened to Christian. When he arrived at his house, his deepest fears were confirmed. A police officer approached him and tried to diffuse the moment. But Randall knew that he had lost his son. He passed the officer and walked straight to his other three children, who were emotionally shocked and in need of their daddy.

What happened?

Two-year-old Christian fell into the Jacuzzi and drowned.

As I sat in Randall's living room and listened to him recount the story, the room funneled into a small sanctuary—as if the story turned his living room into a tiny chapel. Randall doesn't rush when he speaks. He delivered a deliberate and thoughtful word, and in that shrinking moment of heaviness and grief I saw his eyes fill up and heard his voice fall soft as this former world-class athlete reached out with his words to touch his little son one more time.

"How can you tell this story without breaking all over again?" I asked. "How can anyone lose a son and continue to be strong for his family?"

He nodded. He'd heard these questions before; I think he

continues to be just as astounded as the person asking the questions with regard to his ability to deal with such deep pain.

"The Lord gives, Tim, and he also takes."

I'd heard those words a thousand times before but never like this, never in this context. Randall spoke with conviction. He offered no trite cliché. It was the truth to which he clung.

"That day," he continued, "I don't really know how I made it through. I don't know how I was able to drive from my house where my kids were, to the hospital where my wife waited for me with Christian. Those weren't my footsteps. God carried me. It was his strength that enabled me to drive to the hospital, that gave me the presence of mind to be exactly what my other children and wife needed me to be at that moment."

At the hospital he found his wife in a room alone with Christian. He still had oxygen tubes in his nose. She held Christian and said she prayed over him just like Paul the apostle had done to the boy who fell out of the window and died. But Christian did not revive like the boy did.

Randall then took Christian in his arms and held him close. As he held him, his little head fell to the side. That was the crushing blow for Randall.

"I knew the only way we'd be able to move on with our lives was to lay Christian down on the hospital bed and walk out of the room."

So, he laid down his youngest child, took his wife's hand, and left.

THANKSGIVING LEADS TO CONTENTMENT

I spent the next several months talking with Randall about how he was able to lay his son down and, in essence, give the situation to God. Randall didn't give me a five-step process he followed. Rather, he gave me a word: *contentment.*

But this contentment he spoke about was not a kind of "God is God and you're not, so be content in that" contentment. It was a life of forming and failing, striving and winning, experiencing pain and victory, and through it all finally understanding that the key to accepting both the good and the bad circumstances of life boils down to living with an attitude of thanksgiving. And thanksgiving leads to contentment.

Randall entered the NFL in 1985 as a second-round draft pick with pride and an "I'll prove I'm the best" mentality. But when he met teammate Reggie White, he learned the faith in God he thought he possessed was nothing more than religious affiliation. Reggie challenged Randall to cultivate a real *relationship* with Jesus. Randall took the challenge and became a disciple of Jesus.

Randall took the path toward spiritual maturity as he listened to players and coaches, like Reggie, who cared for him and loved Jesus. Over time, his ego diminished even as his NFL star rose and peaked in one of the finest seasons by a quarterback in NFL history. People recall Randall's demeanor that year, how much time he took talking to the media, how kind and engaging he was with them, how he seemed to emote surreal peace and tranquillity.

Randall will tell you it was a year living in the blessing of God. He will also remind you how the next season he lost his starting position to Brad Johnson and then was shipped to Dallas where he rode the bench behind Troy Aikman. He finished his career in 2000 with the Baltimore Ravens going 2–0, serving mostly as a backup.

He will tell you those years following his best work as a quarterback, he served behind the scenes, mentoring guys like Rod Woodson and Ray Lewis. He will tell you how just when you think life looks set up for you, just when you think—as was his case—you might be the next starting quarterback for the Dallas Cowboys, God shows you the real reason why he has you where he does.

But most of the time, we fail to see it. We're too busy striving. Too busy filling our plates with the things *we* want. The needs of the kingdom? We'll worry about those on Sunday or Wednesday or at Christmas. Life lessons can be learned only when we live with our eyes open and turned upward and outward, not on ourselves.

Thanksgiving does not come easily to us. Though we devote a single day and an extended weekend to memorialize the concept of thanksgiving, the rest of the year spins into a web of personal scheming to gain more for ourselves. The drive to have more strikes down the posture of thanksgiving as we chase our own tails in the never-ending cycle of self-satisfaction.

Randall learned how to trust *God* when his life situations did not make human sense. He learned, in essence, to look sideways at any situation. That's where he finds God's handiwork. When we look at life sideways, we're more able to see God's reason (as if he needed any) for what he's up to. Those difficult years of disappointment reinforced Randall's faith. He recognized God working within him and his circumstances behind the scenes, and he learned to accept God's sideways assignment—that mentoring assignment, that servant assignment.

Knowing that God controls those situations with the intent to grow you in a way you never imagined engenders contentment—a characteristic that grows from the sweet root of thanksgiving.

LESSONS FROM A TOOL SHED

Randall's sideways glance at God is perhaps not the whole of the story. We can say he looked sideways at God to make our point: when tragedy strikes, look *around* the circumstance for its meaning. But we struggle with this. Often the circumstance looms too large, or the residual pain from the circumstance stings too much, and we tire of hurt.

Perhaps Randall wasn't looking at God sideways; perhaps he wasn't looking *at* God at all. Maybe he was *living within* God. Maybe his relationship with God had grown so sweet and close that when tragedy struck he saw only God surrounding him, carrying him. He was *in* God, and that position determined his reaction to Christian's passing.

God does not drift on a far-off plain—a deity waiting for us behind a curtain in a cathedral or a church building. He is a being with whom we can communicate, and if we stretch our imaginations, we can climb inside him.

I climb in *and* out of God. I climbed inside him when I walked beneath a deciduous canopy deep in the Hudson Valley of New York. On the outside the trees were only beginning their fall fade. The brisk morning beckoned, so I walked through its breezes to the edge of the wood. I climbed down the granite staircase and, once beneath the canopy, stood motionless—struck with awe.

Below the tall green tops of maple, poplar, and oak stood another canopy of glowing gold and orange. These smaller trees burned with color; their slender ashen trunks were tangled up and into their wonderful inferno.

Beyond the grove stood a sheer cliff. It rose immediate and

sharp, towering over the trees. The waking sun struck the craggy bluff behind the grove and lit it up like a quiet firework of autumn delight.

Joy is like the glowing little trees—shouting color though unseen by most. On this morning I found a piece of God—joy—as I looked along the pointing finger of beauty.

For me, in this moment of being *in* God, I found joy.

I wonder what Randall found. Peace?

I climbed out of God during the same week. I woke early and cracked open my books, breathed deeply, and scuttled around my Greek, poking here and there in the ancient language to find God-clues. I studied a word and then a passage in his Word. I prayed, then sang, and then studied some more. I dug little trenches, encircling the concept of humility, and wondered where God kept its mysteries.

The time was brief but deep. I felt as if I'd climbed that craggy cliff behind the grove of trees to catch a glimpse of God from a safe distance. I studied, observed, and returned to the grove below to drown some more in his joy—in him.

"You get one experience of a thing when you look along it," wrote C. S. Lewis, "and another when you look at it."[1] He suggested that we should always learn from both perspectives, but that in certain cases one perspective gives us a truer experience.

Lewis explains this concept using the example of a boy falling in love with a girl. When they spend time together the whole world appears different. A scientist might look at the situation and describe why the boy feels as he does, noting the biological and chemical reactions occurring within his brain. The boy feels nothing biological; he simply feels love. The difference, according to Lewis, is being *in* something (looking along) or *outside* something (looking at). What Lewis describes in his essay is perspective.

When we are children, something spectacular exists—an unhindered naïveté that allows us to believe that our rocket ship takes us to the footsteps of heaven. Or that jolly Saint Nick squeezes into our chimneys. Or that pulling our blankets tight around our faces and closing our eyes hard enough and long enough keeps the monsters under our beds from seeing us.

Each instance of life—each conversation, encounter, friend, or hiding monster—provides a new perspective. We see things in new ways. Ways in which we never expected or appreciated but ways in which we can't imagine being without. The older we get, the more we start to see *along* and *at* life. Being in it and outside it all at once, we find that our perspectives become more complete.

In the case of God, I believe the truer experience is *looking along*.

I think that we must take great pains to look along God, lest our heads inflate too much with observations and ideas and book stuff. And yet we must observe, we must push on him with our minds, for the harder we push, the farther we are able to walk into the golden canopy—struck to our knees with awe, caught in holy epiphany.

SKEWED PERSPECTIVE

While I was working on Randall's book, I met a couple, Amber and Seth, from northwestern Arkansas. Both are talented writers, daytime professionals, and parents. Seth was writing a blog series that dealt with big questions: What does it really mean to be blessed?

Why do some people who "do everything right" still suffer? How do we live in the tension of blessing and suffering as children of God?

At once I wanted to contribute to the conversation. My blossoming friendship with Randall, along with my digging into his story at length, had begun to stretch my view of God to an almost uncomfortable length and depth. I found myself in a constant state of thankfulness for all the blessings bestowed on my family.

But why was I blessed and others weren't? Are we to pray for blessing and yet remain content if God decides *not* to bless with what we've asked of him?

This morning, after an unpleasant breakfast at Waffle House, my friend Brian and I talked about the *so that* of our faith. He asked, "Do we feed the poor and help the helpless *so that* our faith is validated? No. Our faith exists *so that* we can give glory to God and to enjoy him forever."

As I mulled over this I wondered whether the same principle applied to writing. Why do I write? My sister, an English major at the time, asked me this exact question.

As a scrawny little freshman, I replied, "Because I have to." And I meant it. I didn't know any better. A teacher teaches; a writer writes.

"It's easy to hold the romantic view now, Tim," some might say. "You've got a book contract."

True, but the *blessing* of publishing is recent. I spent my twenties writing poetry and songs and touring the country in a van, playing small music venues. I still write because of a mysterious compulsion to hammer away at words and ideas all day, but now I possess the great advantage of age and experience. I am *blessed* to be able to do what so many spend years wishing and working for—to be a published author.

I am *blessed* to stay home with my wife and our three pixie-daughters, to help teach them, to be around. It's not romantic, and we don't have wads of cash lying around. Quite the contrary. Did I pray to be able to work from home and write and homeschool my pixies? Yes. If God did not allow that to happen, would I live embittered toward God, resentful I didn't get what I asked of him?

I honestly don't know. I was happy before all this: running my landscape company, playing music on the side at local venues, and writing poetry. Wasn't I?

When I moved to Atlanta seven years ago to pursue writing full time, I wrote for free. I still take writing jobs that suck the life out of me so that I can pay the bills and keep writing full time. But every day I remind myself, and my pixies remind me as well, of the blessing it is to be with them, to work as a writer, to have a house, and to have an old Land Rover we were blessed to rebuild so it could keep us poor by guzzling gas. Every day I whisper, "Thank you, God."

I feel as if I am only now learning how to be *content*.

But what if God takes it all away tomorrow? Will I tear my clothes and weep and throw ash all over myself? Probably. Randall told me he looks at his time with Christian as an incredible blessing. God allowed him and his family to have Christian for that time. Rather than resent God for taking his son, he's thankful for the time, brief though it was.

I can only pray that if God ever takes away, I can be as thankful then as I am now. It's difficult to look at friends who find success (as the world defines success) and do nothing special with regard to their spirituality, especially if you believe you are doing everything right. I can relate. But this is what I meant earlier with the *so that*. We don't do things right—we don't live right—*so that* we find success. Rather, we pray for prosperity spiritually and financially and civically[2] and follow Jesus regardless of the outcome.

In the book of Jeremiah the prophet gave the people of Israel a message from God. At the time Israel existed within the confines of Babylon. The people lived as exiles, aliens in a foreign land, and all by the hand of God. Yet God comforted them with these words:

> Build houses and settle down; plant gardens and eat what they produce. Marry and have sons and daughters; find wives for your sons and give your daughters in marriage, so that they too may have sons and daughters. Increase in number there; do not decrease. Also, seek the peace and prosperity of the city to which I have carried you into exile. Pray to the LORD for it, because if it prospers, you too will prosper.[3]

God told the Israelites to be content in a foreign place. Don't complain because of dashed expectations. Make the best of the situation and accept it. Tough news for the Israelites who were hoping for a short exile, but God, in his discipline, also brought relief and showed them a plan. Before this letter from God, the Israelites weren't allowed to marry and national extinction seemed imminent. God allowed them to strike up new relationships, however. All was not lost.[4]

It's easy to lose sight of God's provision when we find ourselves in unfamiliar territory. Like the Israelites, we desire the comforts and peace that accompany the familiarity of home. God directed the Israelites toward an understanding of contentment within discipline.

Far from home they must rely on his goodness. They must trust. That hard word and harder action.

I look at some folks and think, *What are they doing that I'm not? Why can't I have a best seller?*

"It's never enough, is it?" Jesus whispers to me in my prayers.

Then he reminds me: "So what if God chooses to bless them?" Jesus' words to Peter ring true in my ears—so what if I let John live forever? Only *you*, follow me.[5]

GOD OF THE RIDICULOUS

How do we live in the daily tension between suffering and blessing as it relates to life on planet Earth and God's so-called control over both? I say "so-called" because many of us see the atrocities in the world and wonder how a loving God can allow this. I don't pretend to know the answer to this question. I am, however, at ease with its lingering mystery. A haunting mystery, really.

As I continued digging my trench into this tension of blessing and suffering, contentment and thankfulness, I discovered how God built a transcendental framework around an ostrich. In Job 39 God responds to Job's impassioned inquiries about his suffering. We don't find God shoving Job farther into the ashes after Job spends much of the book screaming out to him, demanding God answer his questions, and cursing the day he was born. Contrary to popular belief, we don't find a cosmic, "How dare ye!" from God. Rather, we find a God who willingly condescends to a crushed and confused man. That God then expounds upon himself.

God also describes the ostrich. She flaps her wings joyfully but doesn't seem to realize how puny they are in relation to, say, those of the stork. She's a bit silly. She's also not very smart. She lays her eggs in the sand where any wild animal can trample them. She's not a good mother either; she treats her young harshly as if she's forgotten that they're hers. All that work to bring her young into the world and she couldn't care less.[6]

Why did God create this foolish and ridiculous bird? Through all her silliness and apparent idiocy, she still shines: "When she spreads her feathers to run, she laughs at horse and rider."[7] One envisions this idiot bird cackling with glee along the desert plain—like an overgrown Road Runner—passing horse and rider with an effortless gait. Beep! Beep!

If we follow the ostrich's dust trail we find in this quirky Old Testament passage a sideways view of God like the one Randall saw. Only now we know it's not a view *at* God. It's a view from within.

He gives us the ostrich for no other purpose than to marvel at her ground speed.

This passage also lists the eagle and the hawk, bloodthirsty displays of avian glory living to themselves, for themselves and God. What can *you* do about the eagle? You spot one and, in youthful exuberance, can do nothing but grab your binoculars because you can only marvel.

It's the same with the leviathan and the behemoth: one symbolizes chaos, the other, ferocity. What can we do with them? Nothing.[8]

What is God telling us about these ridiculous and glory-laden creatures?

I am the God of the ridiculous. I am the God of chaos. I am the God of awe. I am the God of the bloodthirsty. I am the God of ferocity.

GOD'S PULLING MYSTERY

Perhaps God did not intend to for us to argue for prosperity or suffering. Perhaps God intends for us, his crowning creative jewel, to rest in his mystery.

Mystery can be exhilarating. It can also be dark and frightening. We love mystery because it draws us toward the light of resolution—that moment of epiphany when we say, "I finally understand."

But with God it's always a "farther up and farther in" pulling. The more we discover, the more he unravels, and the more mystery we must live with.

God's mystery draws us toward *him*. All of us respond differently to this drawing of mystery. Either we will deride God because of his mystery or we will praise him, clinging to the unknown. We have a choice.

I think we choose praise when we learn to live in contentment. Living content, however, does not mean that we live emotionless. Like Job, we can rip our clothes and heave ash upon our heads and wail when we encounter affliction—all while praying, "The LORD gave, and the LORD has taken away."[9] We must learn to live captivated by the mystery of God—within him—if we desire to understand how to live a contented life in the midst of suffering.

Life looks different from the vantage point of mystery. An ostrich runs, an eagle soars, and the hawk hunts in view but out of reach. No point, just glory. Our suffering stamps around like the ostrich, dumb and idiotic, but ready to spread its feathers and run. And here is where we choose. We choose to pray, "Lord save me *from* this!" or "Lord, save me *through* it."

In the Garden of Gethsemane Jesus asked for the cup to be

passed from him. Yet he drank deep the cup of the cross. And there, on the other side of the gory wood, the brilliance of his salvation shone for each of us. His glory came through the cross. His glory yet comes, through you and me. Through the soaring and the stamping, his glory comes—through the contented life, through the wailing life.

THE WAIL OF CONTENTMENT

When I shared these thoughts with my friend Seth and his wife, Amber, she took issue. "You've given me something to think about," she said. "I've got plenty of friends who have always encouraged me to read Job when I'm feeling low, which enrages and confuses me.

"When I read Job, I *do* find a cosmic 'How dare ye!' from God. I see Job, a man who has finally broken—who is miserable and depressed and questioning the fact that the Law says those who do right are blessed and those who do evil suffer. And instead of giving answers, God responds, 'I'm sorry, did you make all this? Are you that awesome? No? Okay then. Shut it.'"

Amber has plenty of reason to be irritated with folks who pitch her Job and tell her things will work for those who trust God. Seth and Amber dealt with a mysterious illness that plagued their youngest son. He couldn't gain weight, and his immune system seemed to be failing. They were stuck in that place between despair and hope.

Christians thrive at throwing clichés at one another in hopes of giving comfort. But we'd do better if we took the time to look into the texts we so flippantly offer when we don't know what else to do.

This dialogue between God and Job looks more like a trial at court. Job seeks vindication and *demands* God give it to him. When God answers Job, "Brace yourself like a man," he is not browbeating Job. Rather, he encourages Job to ready himself with all the human might he can muster so he can somehow comprehend how wide and how deep, how magnificent and unearthly God is.

I had always interpreted this section much as Amber did: "Okay, little man, now that you've stated your quibbling inquiry and your pleading for vindication, I will tell you how great I am and you will take it like a man."

But this is not God's posture at all. It's as if Job hurls every rock of pain and sorrow and confusion at God, and God responds with compassion: "Okay, my beloved child, let me help you understand. Brace yourself, and use all your human faculties to comprehend what I'm about to tell you. I think you'll find comfort."

I believe God expects us to flail and wail and throw glass at the sky and demand to know what is going on. Grace and glory are real, but they're umbrellas covering us as hell falls, not grappling hooks pulling us out of pain. The people who offer those sentiments, though well intentioned, have never suffered or fail to grasp God's overwhelming depth—which all of us do to some degree.

Of course God works all things for the good. But how does knowing that help Seth and Amber now? It does provide a beam of hope—a sliver of brilliance. But in the meantime, they wade through tears and doubt. There is no real answer for suffering other than flinging our rage and unrest at God.

Some years ago a few friends visited me at college. During the visit Erica received a phone call. She stood motionless, ended the call, and began to cry. One of her friends, a recent high school graduate, ran through his second-story window to his death on the street below.

Several months later I sensed Erica was struggling with the suicide of her friend. I grabbed a paper bag, filled it with oranges, and took her up to the Rock—a camping spot a bunch of us frequented on a ridge along the Horseshoe Trail near the Pennsylvania State Game Lands. The actual rock is a massive boulder about the size of an old VW Vanagon. When we got there, I handed the bag to Erica and told her to throw every orange at it while screaming her emotions to God.

Erica followed the directions and emptied the bag, pulp and peels smashed all over the boulder and ground. I didn't promise her an outcome—only the tangible act of releasing her anger, confusion, frustration, and pain. That much she accomplished. Erica flung herself at God that night at the Rock and lived to tell about it.

When we fling ourselves into God, we fall into him, and it feels like dying. But when we land, we are in him. We must remember not only what God said to Job but also what he didn't say. And here true comfort lies.

He didn't tell Job that he's going to get zapped because of what he said: "I will speak out in the anguish of my spirit, I will complain in the bitterness of my soul."[10] No, God *allows* this.

He's big enough to take our hurling accusations at him. He's big enough to hear us curse the day we were born—as Job did—because of our calamity. He's big enough to listen as we wallow in despair. He's big enough to blow us away with the depth of his being in a transcendent effort to comfort us.

And indeed, Job found comfort.

"My ears had heard of you," Job said after God finished his big "I'm awesome" speech, "but now my eyes have *seen* you. Therefore I despise myself, and [find comfort] in dust and ashes."[11]

Chapter 7

A Barbed Wire Horizon

UNDERSTANDING HOW TO FORGIVE
AND SAYING THE WORDS

If you don't hunt it down and kill it, it'll hunt you down and kill you.
—FLANNERY O'CONNOR

Into each life some rain must fall,
Some days must be dark and dreary.
—HENRY WADSWORTH LONGFELLOW, "THE RAINY DAY"

People to whom sin is just a matter of words, to them salvation is just words too.
—WILLIAM FAULKNER, *AS I LAY DYING*

Grandma was picking worms off tobacco leaves from the time she could walk. When she wasn't combing through the fields for bugs, she and the rest of the women in the family busied themselves in the kitchen, snapping green beans or frying something.

On the farm the women served the men supper and waited until they finished eating before sitting down to the meal. Until she died, anytime Grandma fixed a meal, instead of sitting, she walked around the kitchen fretting about whether she had too much flour in the gravy or whether the biscuits were overcooked. She allowed herself to sit only after our plates were full, and we reassured her that everything tasted perfect. And of course it always tasted perfect—throw enough fatback in something and sure enough, it tastes good.

Every now and again she piped up with a story from the farm if one of us prompted her. But never in a fond way. "Just the way it was back then," she said. That code phrase excused her dad and brothers for physically and verbally abusing her. When Grandma turned sixteen, she moved north to Washington, DC. There she met Wade Dallas Locy, my grandpa.

For most of his working life Grandpa drove streetcars (and later buses) for the DC transit system and also painted houses. When he was growing up, his family situation wasn't much better than Grandma's. Rough people, rough times, rough lives.

Grandma grew up in the tobacco fields of Virginia before escaping to DC. Marrying Grandpa didn't make life any easier. On occasion, he shared the same backwoods mentality that had allowed her brothers to treat her the way they did. Add to that Grandpa's drinking and womanizing and her already fragile view of herself, and the world around her cracked further. Except when talking about her kids, grandkids, and great-grandkids, she had a hard time finding anything positive to say. Her world was broken, and she could see only the cracks.

Once their kids were gone, my grandparents retired to a little town not more than forty miles from the tobacco fields Grandma once worked. In their new lives they served in the local church and helped take care of my brother and me. During summer break from school, we climbed into Grandpa's pickup and rode the fifteen minutes from our house to his. Grandma would have an eggs-bacon-potatoes-biscuits-gravy-milk breakfast ready for us.

Grandpa kept us entertained during the day. We played Wiffle ball together or challenged each other to checkers. Some days we went fishing, sitting together and complaining about the fish getting away. Other days, we just ran errands.

On Christmas Eve my dad and uncles would tell stories about growing up with my grandpa. "The old man was so mad, he came at me on the steps. I ducked, and he punched a hole right through the wall," one of them would say. And everyone would laugh at the idea of three raucous boys causing so much trouble. We laughed harder at the old man, as they called him, reacting in these fits of rage that always backfired and caused even more trouble.

The old man they reminisced about over sweet tea and Toll House cookies was a lot different from the one I knew. Sure, he still had a bit of a temper and he was always a little cranky, but it seemed to run in the family. He never raised a hand at me and never threw a cross word my way. Every time he saw me, he told me he loved me. He taught me how to hammer a nail, cut the yard, and bait a line. He let me sit on his lap and steer the truck around the block. He took me to the barbershop for haircuts and shopping with Grandma for school clothes. When all the work for the day was done, we sat on the front porch and he taught me the art of whittling nothing.

A WORLD OF RESTITUTIONS

As I grew older and began to steer my own car, we hung out less. But in the summers I still showed up at least once a week to mow his yard and work around the house. For my twenty-first birthday, he sent me a card with some money and a well wish. On the right-hand side of the card, near the fold and out of the way, he wrote Proverbs 5.

"My son, pay attention to my wisdom," the proverb starts and then continues:

> The lips of the adulterous woman drip honey, . . .
> but in the end she is bitter as gall. . . .
> Keep to a path far from her, . . .
> lest you lose your honor to others
> and your dignity. . . .
> At the end of your life you will groan, . . .
> You will say, "How I hated discipline!
> How my heart spurned correction!
> I would not obey my teachers
> or turn my ear to my instructors."[1]

These words seemed a reflection on his mistakes and a gentle warning for me.

As long as I knew him, Grandpa lived in a world of restitutions, living the last part of his life making up for the first part. Telling his grandkids how much he loved us because he didn't tell his kids enough, spending time with us to make up for lost time with his own sons, serving at the church to prove to God he was serious about his faith this time, and sending me proverbial warnings he wished he had heeded. I think he finally started to figure out that the old time religion he had been singing about all those years might not be the way God had it planned for him.

When I was twelve, my mom and dad drove us all the way from Virginia to Canada to see Niagara Falls. We were still in the driveway unpacking the yellow Oldsmobile 88 that drove us there and back when the kitchen phone rang, telling us that Grandpa was in the hospital—a stroke.

Over the next several weeks our family made the hour trek to the Roanoke hospital to visit Grandpa in rehab. He worked hard at recovering the movement and strength in his left side, and after he started showing signs of progress, they sent him home. After a while things were close to normal for him, but one Sunday after church he tripped as he was leaving the Country Cookin' restaurant and broke his hip. After that he never fully recovered and for the next ten years he spent most of his days in a La-Z-Boy chair, clicking through his programs on TV.

My grandma, the ever dutiful, long-suffering companion, tended his every need. She washed the hands that had once hit her. She cleaned the mouth that had yelled at her. She bathed the body that had betrayed her.

Sure, part of it was duty, but part of it was deeper than that. In her own way, I think she somehow managed to forgive my grandpa for all he'd done to her. She had two choices: forgive or soak in bitterness, leaving an old man to die. So she plowed through the work of forgiving him just like she worked the farm.

One by one, day by day, Grandma inspected the tobacco leaves and plucked off the worms. If she didn't, the worms would eat through the leaves and destroy the crop. On the farm you do your part by picking off the worms, tilling the soil, pulling the weeds. But other things have to happen: the sun needs to rise and the rain needs to fall. You work and you wait. It's an active and passive relationship. I think Grandma's view of forgiveness looked a lot like her work on the farm. She worked at forgiving Grandpa through serving him, but she passively let God do some work in her life and his.

How much of forgiveness is just stick-to-itiveness? If we're committed to someone—truly committed—it seems we have no choice but to forgive that person. That's why it feels like work, just as any relationship can at times feel like work. When my grandma said, "For better or for worse," I'm not sure what she expected. But I bet she couldn't have predicted the "for worse" parts.

It didn't matter. Maybe it was generational. She had to stick it out because that's what folks did back then. But I wonder whether it was deeper. Did she have a sense of love that was rooted in commitment and not just reciprocal, emotional feelings?

Philosopher Soren Kierkegaard talked about this idea, calling the commitment an absurdity. It is a wonderful kind of absurd, though, an absurd that gives us joy and strength. The only way we can live in this absurdity is through the recognition that all things are possible through God. So when we live in the wonderful absurdity, we rest fully on faith in God. In our commitment, Kierkegaard said, we find our identity. In this we find purpose in life that keeps us from falling into despair. It seems to me that repeating the same thing again and again—bathing, feeding, cleaning up after an old man—every day would lead to despair. Yet Kierkegaard argued the opposite. In the commitment we find meaning.[2]

WRESTLING TO FIND PEACE

Heather and I had been married only a couple of years when we bought our first house, a little Cape Cod. One spring day, I was working in the backyard when Heather walked out with the phone. "Your family called, and I think your grandpa isn't going to make it. They want us to come over," she said. We dropped everything and rushed to the care home where he had lived the last couple of months.

"This is it," the nurse said as we sat by his bedside, waiting for the inevitable. Most of the family had gathered, and we whispered in his ear that we loved him. No more to say, he rested while Grandma adjusted his blanket.

We buried him on a sunny afternoon in a cemetery off Route 221. In the distance I could see the Blue Ridge Mountains where he and I used to sit and wait for fish. The grandsons marched the casket over the grass to his final resting place. We all cried our final goodbyes while somewhere he rejoiced.

Those last ten years of his life he spent sitting in pain, wishing he could go hunting or walking or just climbing behind the wheel of his truck and driving the Parkway. I always wondered whether God kept him on earth so long to make him suffer for all the wrongs he committed in his life or to give him time to make up for them.

In some ways, I think God granted him a second chance. His grandkids gave him a new perspective on life and what it meant to love. His sickness gave him a new perspective on what it felt like to be loved, even by someone whom he had so painfully wronged. Through it all he felt forgiveness from those he hurt, and maybe he finally forgave himself.

All those years he wrestled to find peace, and then in those final breaths, God gave it.

BENNY HILL AND THE BARBED WIRE HORIZON

When I wasn't at my grandparents' house, I ran around in the woods that outlined our yard. Each day a pack of us climbed trees, built forts, and gave Ryan Franks a hard time. Around dusk someone's mom would yell, "Dinner!" and we all scattered home to eat our vegetables, clean behind our ears, and scrap our way in and out of bed.

Some nights I camped outside with my neighbor. Roughing it, we pitched a tent to the side of his house and ran an extension cord from the garage to the tent so we could hook up an old black-and-white TV and watch Benny Hill reruns on PBS. Once we knew our parents were asleep, we walked the neighborhood, ringing doorbells and diving into ditches. As morning grew close, we burrowed into our sleeping bags and repeated off-color jokes we heard at school, cracking up at punch lines neither of us understood.

I lived in a little town called Goode. It was the barbed wire horizon of Route 668 set in the foreground of the Blue Ridge, mainly filled with old farmland, middle-class homes, and the Goode Country

Crossroads Store where I held my first job stocking beer and pumping gas. Goode was not much of anything except landscape.

Our family lived in a stone-and-wood ranch house built by my dad. I took the room at the back of the house directly across the hall from my parents' bedroom. Sometimes I could hear my parents talking in their bedroom at night as I drifted off. Mainly their conversation was small talk, family gossip, and the accounting of the day.

One night when I was around eight, I woke up to hear my parents talking. My dad seemed to be on the phone and relaying his conversation to my mom.

"He says he is coming over to shoot me," Dad said.

"What?" she cried.

"He says he has a gun and is going to come over and shoot me," he repeated.

I eavesdropped on the rest of the conversation the best I could, although I don't remember much else. From what I could piece together, my dad was having an affair. I took that to mean he was spending a lot of time with the Man with the Gun's wife. That man never came over with a gun. I guess my dad talked him down. I fell back asleep and kept the overheard conversation to myself.

The next day it rained. Dad walked across the street and mowed the lawn of a neighbor's house. I took my brother into my room and shut the door, and we played by ourselves while Mom paced the house, wondering what to do.

I didn't realize it then, but with the ring of the green Bell Systems telephone that sat on the nightstand next to the bed my parents shared, our family changed. As far as I care to know, this death threat was an isolated incident, but the affair was not. For the next fifteen years the curse of adultery elbowed its way into my parents' marriage.

"You need to do a better job of meeting his needs. Fix this," one of the pastors in our church counseled Mom. I'm not sure whether she believed him, but I don't think the advice mattered much anyhow; she was too scared to do anything except stay. *Keep the family together and protect the boys,* she thought. These ideals became something to cling to while Dad and the church convinced themselves it was better to look good than be good.

Our Southern faith taught us to smile, sing all four verses of the hymns, and keep our sins to ourselves. So, other than the church gossip-tree, no one really knew what was going on with our family.

One time when I was a little older, my mom and I stopped at the grocery store. We pulled into the fire lane so she could run in while I guarded the car. As she got out of the car, she paused. "What would you think if your dad and I weren't married anymore?" she asked.

"I wouldn't like it," I replied.

At the time, she had no idea I heard that call and I have no idea *why* she asked. But I know she wanted me to give her permission to leave. Although I believed what I said, I always regretted not giving her the freedom to make the choice she wanted.

THE DECAY OF SECRETS

The secret stayed inside our house until the time my little brother left for college. Something changed once we boys were out of the house. Mom finally found the courage to leave. Kierkegaard didn't know my mom; every day she stayed in that house, she lost a little bit of her identity, and enough was enough.

I imagine "good-bye" was all she had to say. He knew what she meant. After a marriage filled with running and hiding and lying, Dad was staring face-to-face with the monster he created, as if seeing it for the first time. It's like the ugly thing showed up one day and caught him off guard. Mom could see it. I could see it. But he never could. I don't know why he couldn't see it before, maybe he had the scales over his eyes the Bible talks about. Whatever the reason, whatever kept him from seeing it, my mom ripped it off that day.

Once Mom left, he saw himself: a selfish, scared, shell of a man standing in the shadows of his mistakes. Then one day on his way to work, a car slammed into his. Dad pulled off to the side of the road and climbed out of the car. He bent down on his knees and cried out to God, "I give up." There on the off ramp of Route 221 and Candlers Mountain Road, he gave his life to Christ in a way that he hadn't before. He gave it fully. No more fighting, no more hiding behind the sins of his father, and no more blaming—only submission.

Dad sought counseling, discovered grace, and gave up his philandering ways. It was too late for his marriage, but for him, it was the beginning of a new life. They never reconciled their marriage, but after a while, the marriage wasn't the point anymore. In the end, her leaving turned out for the better.

As he sometimes does, God used the finality of a broken marriage to heal. Dad's salvation rested on her leaving. Had she stayed with my dad, he might not have changed. She left to free herself, but in a way her leaving freed him.

EVAPORATING INNOCENCE

As I grew older, those long and humid Virginia days felt shorter. The feeling of safety I once felt in my grandfather's truck or in the back-woods disappeared. Not like a magician makes a quarter disappear but more in a vaporizing sort of way, my innocence evaporated into the heavens.

The morning after that phone rang, I hopped out of bed and landed on the shards of shattered innocence that surrounded me. It had to happen. No one exists in those childhood summers forever. We grow up. Move out of the house. This is the way the world works, and it's fine as long as we learn how to navigate it.

Yet I couldn't quite figure out how to work the compass. The world seemed to point me in all directions. And I made a decision to keep the phone call to myself, not letting on that I knew. Like my mom, I kept it inside until one night in high school I couldn't hold it in anymore. I confronted my parents about it. My dad made a couple hundred excuses, but eventually he apologized and swore it was an isolated incident. Of course, I knew it wasn't, but I accepted his apology and that was all we ever said on the subject until after the divorce.

When I first learned of the affair, I couldn't quite figure out what it meant. Church taught me that sex outside marriage was wrong, so no way was Dad having sex with other women. For years I thought he was hanging out with these women and just eating ice cream or maybe hitting the Putt-Putt for a quick game of miniature golf before heading home.

About the time my parents made me start using deodorant, I

pieced everything together. There's a pretty good chance that a man doesn't threaten to kill you for eating a bowl of Rocky Road with his wife. Once I knew what an affair involved, I began questioning every action my dad took. I noticed that the car was in a different spot from where he left it the night before or that when mom was out of town, he took a lot of calls in the other room. I noticed the inside jokes exchanged between him and the woman in the store. Sometimes my thoughts were the paranoia of a kid who watched too much *Magnum, P.I.*, and other times I think I was right.

Regardless of the validity of my thoughts, this mentality made it hard for me to trust. With a head full of doubt, I lay in bed almost every night until I was seventeen, wondering whether my parents would stay together or split. I wondered whether my dad was lying to me about other stuff. And I worried about the stability of our family. Would this be the affair that finally broke up my parents? Had mom finally had enough? Would she pull into the fire lane at the grocery store and ask me again?

I felt guilt for not telling my mom. And I was scared and confused. How could someone who loved us so much do such a thing? It made no sense.

For better or worse, I became a product of that night. Not that it defined me, but because I define so much by it. My grandmother was a cynic because of her past, and that affected my dad's perspective and then mine. For a long time I recalled that night and thought, *Oh, so that's how the world works.* Everyone lies about something. Never open up fully; keep some parts to yourself.

LOST BEARINGS

In my thirties I realized that how I navigated the world was off course. My past shaped my perspective too much. That night explained too much of who I was. So, I set out to fix it by doing the same thing my dad did when my mom said good-bye. I stared my past down and confronted it. I stopped hiding, and for the first time, I reached out to someone other than my wife and shared about my past and the reason for my parents' divorce.

Close friends sat quietly as I explained life details they had never heard before. I explained how much it screwed me up, and I asked them to understand. I have good friends because no one laughed at me, no one judged me, and no one seemed to blame me. Something amazing happened: I felt freedom I hadn't felt before. I felt the love of my friends, and I felt an openness I didn't know could exist.

I climbed out of bed the morning after that phone call and stepped on pieces of brokenness. For some reason, my instinct was to just keep walking around, letting the shards poke my feet. I guess it made sense. Walking in the pain worked as a reminder not to follow in my dad's footsteps. But as I grew older and as the situation moved farther away, the natural thing to do wasn't to walk around with the shards of pain poking my feet but to reach down and brush them off. Grace—not pain—now serves as the reminder.

Who knows why the Locy men behaved the way they did? Maybe it was pride or pain or immaturity or all that working together to form a pattern of self-destructive behavior. It's hard to fully understand the *why* behind something like this. There are too many factors. And understanding the why doesn't help. In fact, it may lead to what C. S. Lewis described as excusing instead of forgiving. When we excuse something we can rationalize why it happened. This keeps us from forgiving.[3]

When I walked around with my broken innocence clinging to my feet, I was walking in bitterness. When I didn't forgive, I was holding on to the pain and repeating the same patterns as my dad and his dad before him. His pride kept him from giving himself fully to my mom and our family. My pride kept me from forgiving him. The pain from his childhood led him to believe lies about himself. My pain from my childhood led me to believe lies about myself. All this kept me from forgiving. My sin wasn't adultery, lying, or betrayal. My sin was not recognizing my sins.

THE BUSINESS OF FORGIVENESS

Forgiveness is hard business. Forgiveness is complex because we human beings are so complex. When someone cuts in front of you in line, he may say, "Sorry about that," and in a moment you forgive him and move on. That type of forgiveness is easy, no level of intro-spection needed. The bigger things take a while. Forgiveness isn't hardwired into our systems.

Often, it's not a single act that needs forgiveness, which compli-cates things further. When my dad cheated on my mom and lied to our family, it wasn't just adultery that needed forgiving. A behavior pattern began to unfold. It wasn't just one lie; it was many. It wasn't just his adultery but the self-loathing that manifested in anger. Soon, it wasn't his betrayal I had a problem with; it was him in general.

Forgiveness became harder because no matter what he did, I felt wronged. When we live in this tension we become angry, and

unfortunately the ones around us feel the weight as innocent bystand-
ers of our unforgiveness. The old joke goes that at work the dad gets
yelled at, so he comes home and yells at his wife, who yells at the
kid, who kicks the dog, who chases the cat. The poor goldfish has no
chance. My pain trickled down and ended up unintentionally hurting those around me.

***

How unique that God forgave us our sins in such a spectacular way.
He sent his Son to this earth, where at the age of thirty-three he
found himself in a garden betrayed by one of his closest friends and
arrested. He was accused of being a liar, and his own people chose
his crucifixion over that of a murderer. He was beaten, spat upon,
and marched through the streets. He was humiliated in front of his
family. He hung on a cross for hours while the guards below him
gambled for his clothes. All that happened while the very weight
of the world rested on his shoulders, slowly killing him. If that
wasn't enough, he spent three days in total separation from God,
his Father.

Not to sound trite, but this sounds a lot like forgiving to me.
It's long and hard and painful. It's a process. We work it like my
grandma worked that field. We pray through it and ask God to
release the pain and the hurt. When we do this, God is faithful, and
one day grace begins to seep in. And if we let grace in, it fills us and
drowns out the hurt.

We must work at forgiveness. If we don't forgive, how can we
experience forgiveness from God? Our lack of forgiveness keeps us

from our heavenly Father. "Forgive us our trespasses as we forgive those who trespass against us," Jesus teaches us to pray. We forgive as we are forgiven; it's all happening together, as in the parable of the debtor. The king forgives the debt, but the debtor doesn't forgive the debt owed him.[4] Who am I to ask Christ for forgiveness without forgiving my dad?

In some ways Grandpa had forgiveness given to him through love. Grandma showed her love and commitment through her dutiful acts and the grandkids through a simple hug and an "I love you." This love did its best to pave the way for grace and began to fill the holes and wounds of his heart.

You can't love in moderation, so you choose to love fully or live in the tension of love and bitterness and distance. Grown now, I look at my kids and know how much I love them, and I know that my dad loves me the same. And no matter how much I love my kids, I realize my love is human and incomplete. But I imagine the perfect love of our heavenly Father. We love because he loved. In that love, we find forgiveness for ourselves, and we pass that on to others. It's not as easy as it sounds, but we try anyway.

***

One Sunday afternoon not too long ago, Dad was visiting, and we went outside on the driveway for a pickup game of basketball with my sons. The game between my dad and me was the same as it was twenty years ago in the backyard of that house in Virginia. I pushed at him as hard as I could, to prove I was strong. He pushed back, to prove he was stronger.

After a couple of games we were both tired and soaked in sweat. We crouched down and rested our hands on our knees.

"My feet hurt," said Dad.

"My knees are killing me," I replied.

We laughed at each other's aching bones, and I looked up and caught his tired eyes. He was just an old man with aching feet who had made a ton of mistakes in life, and like his father before him, he was paying penance. I was a grown man, with creaking knees, whose life was filled with mistakes.

I looked at my kids and thought about all the horrible parenting they had waiting for them. I prayed the good would outweigh the bad. I hoped that with all my mistakes I would one day visit their houses for a pickup game of basketball with them and their kids.

That day in my driveway, grace filled the basketball court, and when I wiped the sweat out of my eyes I saw forgiveness. For a couple of minutes, God gave me the total peace that my grandfather discovered only on his deathbed.

In the end, sometimes that's the best we can hope for on this earth. Three generations of family, making peace with the past, shooting baskets in the driveway.

God, forgive me. God, help me forgive.

Chapter 8

The Weightlessness of Love

REALIZING WHEN OUR HEARTS CHANGE, OUR MINDS FORGET THE HURT

Forgiveness is not an occasional act; it is a permanent attitude.
—MARTIN LUTHER KING JR.

Above all, love each other deeply, because love covers over a multitude of sins.
—PETER THE APOSTLE

Peter came up and said to him, "Lord, how often will my brother sin against me, and I forgive him? As many as seven times?" Jesus said to him, "I do not say to you seven times, but seventy-seven times."
—MATTHEW 18:21–22

It was one of those discussions you never forget. The winter sun gleamed into the family room. My (Tim's) brother, Jon, sat on the couch across the room. My father walked in and sat on a chair to my left.

"Whatcha talking about?"

"Nothing. Forgiveness," I said.

He didn't answer.

"Dad, what is forgiveness? How does it work? Is it a process? Or is it an event, etched in time?"

For the last thirty years my dad has served as the pastor of adult care at my former home church. Among his teaching duties, he also counsels people, marries them, holds their hands through times of grief, visits sick folks in the hospital, and performs graveside duties. His job, in a nutshell, is that of compassion giver. At least, that's what I call it.

"Forgiveness," he said as he looked across the room into the sunlight, "is a singular event in the form of a word given to someone who has wronged us. It does not *erase* the transgression that necessitates the need for forgiveness right away. Rather, it allows the process of healing to begin."

My brother and I didn't speak. It was a father-son moment when the father pours wisdom upon the sons' heads while the sons remain still—cupped hands to the side to collect the drops.

"Forgiveness," he continued, "must take place first in the heart. The heart is the wellspring of our souls. We cannot heal unless our hearts reach out in love and release the transgressor of the wrong."

Then he said something that surprised me.

I've often grimaced at the Christian cliché "forgive and forget."

I didn't believe it true for the same reasons my father gave—forgiving someone doesn't erase what he or she did. Our actions carry consequences, and those consequences remain. But my dad looked toward the floor, deep in thought, gestured with his hands, and said, "But when the heart forgives, the mind no longer remembers."

It is not of ourselves that we can forgive.

But forgiveness seems so far away. The Sandy Hook calamity, the complex circumstance of lengthy deceit and betrayal such as Jason endured as a young boy, sexual abuse, verbal cruelty—I don't need to lengthen this list. We all know it. How can we ever forget? *Should* we ever forget?

The light warmed to a deep orange as the sun hung over the west hills, soft and covering. For days over the Christmas break I'd canvassed my friends around bonfires and kitchen tables. "What is *forgiveness?*" I'd ask. And now midst the chaos of ten grandchildren, turkey, and presents, my brother and I listened to the sounds of forgiveness uttered forth in simple—yet stern—words from our father. His sounds shaped into words and fell into thoughts and ran over my insides like the tucking winter sun.

Was this it? Forgive and forget?

It was Christmas, but the whole nation mourned. When that lone gunman entered Sandy Hook Elementary School in Newtown, Connecticut, and killed twenty children and seven adults (including himself), our nation regained a conscience.

Then one cold Connecticut morning, Emilie Parker's father held a press conference. He pleaded for us, as a nation, to remember his daughter as a real little girl who loved to act like she was in charge. He told a weeping nation how she loved life and how if she were still alive, she would have been the first person to offer comfort to those who'd experienced such deep loss. Next he did something strange. He offered the most precious gift a person can give to another person with his words.

He forgave the gunman.

What did his forgiveness accomplish?

It did not erase what happened. Twenty-eight people, including the gunman's mother, still lay dead. Forgiving the gunman did not end our grieving. It did not answer the myriad questions swirling around in everyone's mind. It did not make everything right.

It did, however, allow a nation to witness a most profound and unearthly love. In our eyes, Adam Lanza did not deserve to be forgiven. He deserved pain and suffering—he deserved a harsher penalty than suicide. And yet in the breath of one word, *forgive,* a moral outlook we don't fully understand entered the national discourse. That same word fell from the lips of the parents who lost their daughters in the Amish school shooting in 2006. God's love stood front and center, but our hearts could not grasp it.

In the Old Testament when God says, "[I] will remember their sins no more,"[1] is he also saying, "I will forgive them fully"? We are not God. We like grudges. And for some reason bitterness tastes good to us. Forgiveness is hard. But hard doesn't mean impossible. Hard here means possible only with God's help, God's strength.

I am teaching my daughters to ask forgiveness when they've wronged one another. I'm also teaching them to forgive freely. Even through tears they are quick to utter, "Will you forgive me?" or "I forgive you." They hug and jump back into Strawberry Shortcake within minutes. They're learning how to engage in the act of forgiveness. As children, they have no problem picking up where they left off in their relationship. Their little minds are still very much governed by their big hearts.

In time, I suppose, that will change. Their behavior will shift in light of the circumstances. Their minds will grow, but I hope not enough to overrule their hearts and their love for one another.

We grow, and too often our hearts shrink. We live like the Grinch, pacing within our caves, hating this and that and him and her, forgetting why we love and who we love. I don't know that forgiveness is a process. I think, rather, it begins as a way of life. It begins, says Kierkegaard in *Works of Love*, when we love one another and then extend toward the heavens.[2] It holds so tightly to God that when the shadows emerge in the form of a gunman or a betraying father, "I forgive" lies on the ready, etched in time, solid. And the road to restitution opens with God's love on the horizon beckoning us onward.

Our little talk ended with the sun behind the rolling horizon and fresh coffee in our cups. "Last week I was talking to a group at church," said my father, wrapping up. "One woman told the story of her young niece who had, for several years, been sexually molested by her uncle. The uncle was sent to prison but was set for release. The niece, grown now, was having trouble dealing with her uncle's release. The woman in my group stopped telling her story and looked up at the rest of us in the room. 'I'll never forgive him, never, for what he did to her.'" That is the heavy struggle of forgiveness. Who can blame her?

My father's report bothered me, but if I'm honest, it saddened me more. I could see this woman pacing in her cave of resentment. What would draw her from her lair? I could see my daughters stepping out from their caves and hugging, and love winning the moment. But this woman couldn't let herself forget. And in her remembering she moved deeper into her cave, away from reconciliation.

Christ invites us to lay down our burdens and to take up his burden. It's light.

But I won't know it's light until I take his word for it and actually give him my burden. I must trust him. If I'm going to lay this bit of bitterness or betrayal or loss at his feet and step into his yoke, I have to trust that it will indeed lighten my load. On a spiritual level then, if I can't trust, I can't forgive. But practically speaking, it's the same. Is there something about you that engenders trust within me so that my lips move and forgiveness dribbles forth? I think this is why so many of us bottle up our feelings of hurt and betrayal—we really don't think our friends and family are trustworthy.

"Why should I forgive my husband, he does this all the time?"

"She's just going to turn around and forget everything she just said. Why should I forgive *her*?"

Round and round we go with reason after reason for not forgiving. We won't be burned twice, not today, not again. But I go back to what my father said about the heart. Many of us get good at saying things devoid of truth, devoid of the heart. We say we forgive, but our hearts cling to the hurt. Without trust, we cannot forgive. It's the trust we develop in our relationships that allows forgiveness to come, like the refreshing spring rains. But what if we could develop enough trust in our Lord that betrayals and hurts get passed over, even though the sting lingers.

Forgiveness, like this, looks like me trusting God that over time, the wound will heal. My heart beats softly for the Lord and my trust in *him* deepens even though you and I may be on shaky ground. At this point, it's his forgiveness in me that works, not my own. I can forgive seventy times seven, as he told Peter and the disciples to do, because I am confident in my own forgiveness. My heart, held by my Lord, helps my mind to forget. I forgive, because he forgave me. Forgiveness *is* hard, but it's not impossible. Maybe we need to first begin with realizing our own need for God's forgiveness. Then our caves of bitterness don't feel so comfortable. Rather, we run out into the brilliance shouting, "I've forgiven because I myself am forgiven."

I want always to step out from my cave. I want always to forgive. And I want always my heart *and* mind to release wrongs. It is as rudimentary as stepping toward the splintered yoke of Christ and as difficult as bearing the gashes of the crushing thorns.

"When the heart forgives, the mind no longer remembers."

Chapter 9

Life as Dance and the Brush Fire of Brilliance

THE IMPORTANCE OF COMMUNION WITH GOD

I will celebrate before the LORD. I will become even more undignified than this, and I will be humiliated in my own eyes.
—KING DAVID

Just living life is not enough. We must know what we are living.
—HENRI J. M. NOUWEN, *CAN YOU DRINK THE CUP?*

Ye blessed Creatures, I have heard the call
Ye to each other make; I see
The heavens laugh with you in your Jubilee ...
—WILLIAM WORDSWORTH, *ODE: INTIMATIONS OF IMMORTALITY FROM RECOLLECTIONS OF EARLY CHILDHOOD*

"The biggest thing I've learned as a parent," my (Tim's) friend Greg once told me, "is how I've returned to infancy. The older I get, the more of a toddler I become, and I see how God loves me, how I am his son. It's like returning to childhood all over again."

It's a universal phenomenon: you marry and have children, and a side of God's brilliance, his beauty, that you've not yet seen, shines into your life. If you can stand the magnificence, you won't just learn; you'll find yourself transformed. That's what this man was saying. That's what I, three-girls-under-five-in, find as not just experience but truth.

As I considered his words, I thought back two days before then. Brielle, my three-year-old, danced for me in her ballerina dress. Back and forth she danced across the living room floor, pitching glances at me to make sure I was watching. And I was.

"You're a beautiful dancer, Brielle. I love when you dance."

"Tanks, Daddy," she said through her toothy grin and endearing lisp.

I wanted to sit there all morning.

I'm God right now, I thought, *caught in the rapture of my child's dance.*

Then I thought, *I'm Tim right now. I should dance more for God.*

You may be thinking: *It's all so melodramatic and quaint, Tim, but I don't have a three-year-old in a ballerina outfit. And even if I did, what about all the other times when she's not dancing?*

That's fair. The other times—when my girls don't dance—pile up like the wheat waffles they love so much but fail to finish. They fight. They disobey. At times they refuse my help, which leads to hurt—falling off a stool or hitting the end of a coffee table or running into a door.

They stamp around doing what they want until they fall. Then they run to me. I scold. I reprimand. I bear-hug them back into peace. They climb onto my lap, restored.

I am a child like that, I thought, *stamping around doing what I please—busy, not dancing, clamoring for the fading jewel of worldly success.*

Peter helps me here. The impetuous apostle, Peter stamped around, saying and doing what he liked. He was like one of the "believers" at the triumphal entry screaming, "Hail, Jesus, King of the Jews." The next week, however, those same people screamed, "Crucify him!" That was Peter, one day committing his undying loyalty; the next, denying the very person he said he loved. Part of me wonders whether Peter thought Jesus was going to bring a *real* sword and overthrow the government like those "believers" at the Jerusalem gate. He was the gung ho hooligan fisherman.

"You shall never wash my feet!"

"Then you have no part with me."

"Where are you going?"

"Where I am going, you cannot follow."

"Not follow? What are you saying? I will follow you into death!"

"Will you really follow me into death, Peter? Even tonight you will disown me before the rooster crows."

Huff and *puff,* and *stamp, stamp, stamp.* But Peter had Christ all figured. Peter played on the couch when he knew he shouldn't.

I am like Peter, a brash child thinking I have it all figured—I have Christ all figured.

When we get things all figured, we stop dancing. We start stamping to the beat of *me.* And that's what Greg was talking about.

Jesus wants us to dance. He wants us to sit with him in the

garden and pray. But we want to cut off someone's ear to prove to him that we're all in.

"Put the sword down, Peter. Just dance."

For a full day I thought of my friend's words and how I, too, understood better how to be a child of God. When I'm not stamping around doing my own thing, I find delight in the faith dance. I clamber up and sit in his embrace.

Being in Los Angeles when I talked to Greg, I walked to the ocean at sunset to ask God what he wanted to tell me as his child, his son. I wanted to dance. I wanted to listen.

The sky was a great conflagration—a brush fire eating up the winter horizon. I stood alone, except for one petite woman some fifty feet from me. She'd left her boots several yards behind her and stood barefoot as the tide rolled up from the spitting whitecap crashes. The wind blew bitterly from the west. How cold the water must have been! But there she stood, in the coal light of the shadowy sunset, her sweatpants sagging in the splashing wet. The water washed up deeper and deeper and covered her calves. As the tide grew stronger, she took steps farther out. As she moved closer I, still in my boots, stepped back.

The sky beckoned both of us, but only she removed her boots and walked toward it.

"What do you want from me, Father?"

"I want you to watch the woman inch closer, in the frigid water, toward the brush fire I lit. I want you to take off your boots and step in the icy ocean and walk toward my glory. I'm not here to scold or reprimand. My glory beckons my children into dance."

I untied my boots and stepped into the water.

***

We dance through life. We stamp through life. We live as children. We grow into our childhood. And God watches. He says, "Dance for me. But if all you can do right now is stamp like a toddler, so be it."

If Jason and I were God, we'd pull our children close whether they dance or stamp. Only one caveat remains: we must step into him, as it were. We must take off our boots and ease into the frigid waters of his love. We must walk farther and farther into him, toward the brilliance of the brush fire sky. When we reach the horizon— where land meets sky—we'll find our Father.

He'll scold and reprimand. He'll kiss and embrace. But we must take the step and walk toward him—into him. When we do, we find the light of the brilliance not so blinding.

But what do we do? We live unto ourselves. We have it all fig- ured out. We don't trust. And our belief? Well, we toss that out with our toddler toys. We're big boys and girls now. We've developed a sanitized faith, one that keeps us out of the frigid waters of the unknown, one that insulates us from those we hurt, those we love, those we hope to know. We'd rather stamp in our basements, alone and in control, than get our sweatpants wet.

In C. S. Lewis's masterpiece *Till We Have Faces*, Psyche says, "The sweetest thing in all my life has been the longing . . . to find the place where all the beauty came from."[1] I see a brilliance weaving throughout my life—like something softly pushing, showing, even illuminating the beauty entrenched in the shadows all around us. I now walk waist deep in the frigid waters and have set my eyes on the horizon, rarely looking back. The deeper I walk into the brush fire horizon, the more I dance, the more beauty I see.

When I hold my daughters before they fall into sleep, I see the brilliance too. I see the horizon burning before me and every decision I make for them, every instance I am forced to discipline, every step I take toward God for them and for my wife and for me moves me deeper until I see that I am waist deep in freezing waters. And in those freezing waters I find something beautiful, even intoxicating— I find beauty in what used to be shadows of my life. My belief grows. I forgive more easily. I don't mind the hard decisions. The further I walk into him, the more beautiful everything I touch becomes.

It's invigorating.

Chapter 10

Living in Delight

GLORIFYING GOD IN ALL WE DO: THROUGH PLAY, IMAGINATION, LEISURE, AND VOCATION

I never did anything worth doing by accident, nor did any
of my inventions come indirectly through accident.
—THOMAS EDISON

Amusements are to virtue like breezes of air to the flame;
gentle ones will fan it, but strong ones will put it out.
—DAVID THOMAS

Men were created to employ themselves in some work,
and not to lie down in inactivity and idleness.
—JOHN CALVIN

Every year we (the Willards) lived in Atlanta, I'd pine for the Christmas season. I love the Northeast in winter. So, following the cold, the snow, and our extended families, we'd take a Great White North Adventure. The first year, the trip proved easeful for my wife and me. That's code for saying we didn't have kids yet. But time marches. Now, three little girls later, we load up our gear and our pixies into a twelve-year-old Land Rover—affectionately called "Ye Ole Rover"—and trek to the Great White North. Easeful, however, no longer applies.

In 2012, Ye Ole Rover needed a few things before she would be able to make the trip: a new water pump and gasket, a new radiator top hose, a good coolant flush, and, oh yes, a new rear suspension. Let's dig in, shall we?

I removed the water pump, which revealed the engine block in all its burly glory. I cleaned the visible—and reachable—section of the block so I could see future leaks and then slapped on the new pump and gasket. Success!

I reassembled everything and rumbled down the street for a test drive. Then, the radiator top hose burst. I replaced it and, *Voila!,* no leaks. I was so pleased with my success I prepared to install the new rear suspension—the one that just arrived.

I would ready the garage and begin in the morning.

Dropping the rear suspension is no joke. I spent four hours trying to lower the axles far enough for the springs to fit into place. I rented a special tool. It didn't work. I readjusted my jack. Nothing. Finally, I did what everyone does when he encounters an impasse while replacing the rear suspension: I sat on the concrete and stared at my wheel hubs for about an hour.

Night fell. I went to bed.

The next morning, as I continued staring at the wheel hubs in the morning drizzle, it dawned on me. *Was it possible I hadn't raised my Rover high enough? No. Could it be?*

So, I cranked Ye Ole Rover higher, higher, and higher. The frame creaked as it raised, and the concrete beneath the jack made uncomfortable crunching sounds.

Two more clicks, got it. My heart pounded.

Once the vehicle settled from the jacking, something beautiful happened.

The rear end fully articulated, and the axle fell almost to the ground.

My new springs fit into place with ease. I shouted and pumped my arms in the cool December rain; Lyric and Brielle, who'd wandered into the garage to see what all the hoopla was about, hooted and hollered with me. They're gearhead pixies. The Rover was ready for the journey north.

TO LIVE IS TO GLORIFY

I feel *alive* when I work on my truck. My mind releases and focuses at the same time. Oil and grime crawl under my fingernails. I don't wash my hands for at least a day, maybe two. I danced that rainy morning when I replaced my truck's suspension. I felt wholeness, glory, and delight.

And that's the point, isn't it? Everything we do, whether in word or deed done as unto the Lord. It's a chance to give thanks and worship God with every bit of our lives, not just during Sunday morning singing. Whether I sit to work on a book as a means to make a living, or whether I mow the grass in order to maintain my yard; whether I play with my girls at the park or lose myself on the north Georgia trails riding my mountain bike—they are all opportunities to worship God. And our motives live wrapped up in these worshipful acts. Our actions extend from our hearts begging the question: *What do our hearts desire?*

Either our hearts will thrive on worship as intended, or we will bend our worship toward ourselves.

We allow so much to escape us: time, intent, and joy. We allow our endeavors to surrender to the zeitgeist, what Yale theologian Miroslav Volf refers to as the spirit of "experiential satisfaction."[1] In a culture that now seeks personal experience as a means to satisfaction, whatever brings pleasure is deemed good. We've shifted from a people striving for something beyond ourselves to pursuing all things for our gratification. We've exchanged the brilliance of a transcendent God for our "mundane affairs."[2]

Is it too much for us to look deeper into how we use our time, to evaluate our motives for the work we pursue and the leisure activities in which we participate? What if our lackadaisical approach to amusement and entertainment held deeper consequences? What if working on my Rover's suspension was, in reality, a gateway into a life of hope and love?

"When we place pleasure at the center of the good life," wrote Volf, "when we decouple it from the love of God, the ultimate source of meaning, and when we sever it from love of neighbor and hope for a common future, we are left, in the words of Andrew Delbanco, 'with no way of organizing desire into a structure of meaning.'"[3]

Meaning—all of us search for it. As Christians, you and I find meaning in our createdness—children of God set upon the earth to glorify him and enjoy him forever. In the beauty of Christ as the Son of God we find the source of all hope. You and I pursue Christ because we love him. Our love fuels our hope of him returning for us in the near future.

But when our love shrinks from the hope of future glory and rests on self-gratification, and it "devolves into the experience of satisfaction, hope disappears as well," wrote Volf.[4]

When to the drizzle of the December morning my daughters joined me in gearhead jubilation, we danced to the music of transcendence. It was music from some *other world*, a world alighting upon the shadows of self-interest. And it felt good; it felt holy; it felt right; it even felt beautiful (if it's possible to feel beauty). Then and there we danced within hope because I was able to persevere, all to the glory of God.

IT FEELS GOOD TO WORK WITH MY HANDS

Think about the world in which we live. Surrounded by glowing rectangles, we've become the idiot society. And by idiot I mean we've slunk into isolation, content to meddle on our screens, download apps, and sit on our couches. We buy things and then throw them away. We forget, long ago in a faraway land, our purchases used to come with a set of "fix it" instructions.

Not so anymore. We sit. We buy. We discard.

Matthew Crawford wrote a *New York Times* best seller titled *Shop Class as Soulcraft*. He suggests, in our land of superslick intuitive computer interfaces, we've drifted away from the agency required to fix or build. Meaning: *we don't work on our cars anymore or much of anything for that matter.* As we've drifted away from agency, we've drifted toward an autonomous existence in a world devoid of psychic friction. Meaning: *we've outsourced our brains and mechanical prowess for a life of ease.*

When I futz around on Ye Ole Rover, I tend toward discipline, detail, and perseverance. I can't swipe an app. I must turn the wrench. I must unlearn the gospel of ease and intuitive interface interaction and relearn what it means to work on something with my hands—to build, sew, seed, prune, saw, stitch, and bleed.

I'm no mechanic, but that's not the point. When I lie on my back in my garage and wrestle a shock off my Rover, when I bust my knuckles on the rotor, I'm interacting with the material things around me. I'm acquainting myself with the world so I can know it better. I'm also engaging my intellect *and* imagination. I'm feeding the contemplative side of my brain through meaningful agency for a purpose outside myself.

The gains from such engagement also benefit me on a personal level. When I grip the tools of this world, when I fix, mend, serve, and build, I build the person within. This is the opposite of what it means to be an idiot.

An idiot, in the classical sense, is a person who does not extend his knowledge outside himself. If I'm an idiot, I stay to myself and care little about acquainting with the world around me in a helpful way and more about my comfort. An idiot is self-centered at best and centered on nothing at worst.

Our leisure time matters to God. We're responsible for it.

Nobody wants a culture full of idiots. But that's what happens when modern civilization runs to the gospel of selfishness. The greed produced by such a culture causes some people to think the right to pursue happiness means "I'm gonna get mine." But it doesn't.

TRUE HAPPINESS

We forget the pursuit of happiness entails a lifelong chase. We don't procure happiness as if it could be purchased at Macy's. Happiness does not culminate in the aggregate of things or the accruement of power.

Happiness, according to the ancient Greeks, extends beyond us, just out of grasp. Only at the end of a pursuit can we evaluate our goal and determine whether we've achieved it. When we can look upon our lives from the vantage point of age and experience, survey all we've accomplished, who we've helped, the causes we've initiated, and the good we've added in creating, *then* we have achieved happiness. When we finally rest on our deathbeds and survey the good we've accomplished, each of us will be able to say, "I finally understand what it means to be happy."

Material possession and emotional satisfaction do not constitute the whole of happiness. They may *contribute* to it, but that is all.

Thomas Jefferson's dream of happiness shot much higher than our current interpretation. Along with other signers of the Declaration of Independence, he dreamed of a land where citizens considered the needs and values of others as greater than their own. They dreamed of a land where, at the end of their lives, citizens would look back and say, "Yes, I did my best *for* the best of those whom I love and for my neighbors." The Greeks would have been proud, at least of Jefferson's initial intent.

Happiness, at least by Jeffersonian definition, works with the community in mind. Each day our work should reflect our desire to achieve something good not only for personal growth but also for society. The forefathers' understanding of happiness looks similar to what God intended our everyday work to be: *an endeavor of beauty and grace in the service of God and others.*

RECONNECTING MY FRAGMENTED SELF

During the week I work as a writer. I build sentences and stack thoughts into epiphanies. But what do I do with my time when I rest the pen? Does a different Tim surface when I close the laptop and head downstairs into the land of my three daughters and wife?

God created man in his own image. Then he set Adam to work and guard the garden.

"Here is my gift to you—this is what you'll do. Some of you will make tents, others will build microchips, and others will paint on canvas. And when you finish, you'll rest your mind and pick up a spade and plant a garden, ride your bike on the mountains, or drag race.

"Remember, whether you teach high school, quilt, or race moto-cross, you do it *all* to me. Like me, you're whole and composite."

For some reason, though, our society likes to fragment people into specific vocations. Oh, you quilt? You must be a mother or a farmer's wife. That's not a real job. Oh, you manage a household, pay bills, and do the books for your husband's LLC? That's not a real job; you don't receive a salary or benefits or all the things indicative of a viable job.

Three challenges face us in our advanced world, and each contributes to our human fragmentation. In the past, work organized around the family unit. Not so anymore. Now our work organizes around companies and governments. Work narrows in definition to paid employment. We look to our work and how far we've climbed the company ladder as a measure of our personal worth.

Next, the labor markets create an imbalanced view of viable work options. If you can't find work in a legitimate market, your work is not valid. So long to wives who help run the family *and* the family business. We don't have a viable market for you (or so the thinking goes). This recent tension has risen to a fever pitch in our culture as women in the media and on the Internet fight over what is viable work and what is not. This tension exists, in large part, due to our conflated definition of work.

So long, freelance artists. No legitimate market exists for you—we just can't fit you into a quantifiable box. Oh, and you, Mr. Minister, your market shrinks the more you waste time discipling people. We can't see the results, and let's be honest, sitting in Starbucks, talking with folks, is just a hip cover for being lazy and not contributing.

Finally, our technologically advanced world relies on industrialization to produce many of the products we consume. The industrial nature of work removes human beings as the subject of the work process, relegating them to mere objects in the industrial mechanism. The worker can choose from different assembly-line jobs where mundane repetition fights with the innate drive to create and feel a sense of worth through accomplishment.

A Thoreau quotation seems appropriate here. The deliberate poet said,

> Most men, even in this comparatively free country, through mere ignorance and mistake, are so occupied with the factitious cares and superfluously coarse labors of life that its finer fruits cannot be plucked by them. Their fingers, from excessive toil, are too clumsy and tremble too much for that. Actually, the laboring man has not leisure for a true integrity day by day; he cannot afford to sustain the manliest relations to men; his labor would be depreciated in the market. He has no time to be anything but a machine.[5]

I fear our culture grinds itself into oblivion. And as a result, we're so spent that our leisure becomes self-centered and mindless, not to mention centered on a screen. But unplugging from the toil of work does not mean turning off intellect and imagination. Our imaginations do not exist so we can numb them, nor do they thrive in such a state. Like our bodies, our imaginations thrive when we use them.

My most refreshing times on a mountain bike come when I carry a Moleskine in my backpack and record all the thoughts bubbling up from the endorphins and white-blood-cell creation of my hill climbing and trail descending. My mind fires while my legs burn. I spend myself and find the euphoria of refreshment, all the while feeding my imagination the openness of the woods, the smell of honeysuckle, and the excitement of blowing through streambeds.

We must also be careful not to think the world of the imaginary is the same as the imaginative. We use the imaginary to escape reality, but we use the "imaginative" as "a gateway to other and better worlds."[6] We must consider, then, how we steward the delight of the imaginative.

Am I espousing some sly narrative to condemn all movie watching and video game playing? Not exactly. I've sat on the couch, exhausted from a day of work and chasing little ones. I know what it feels like to be spent. It's a matter of stewardship, of redeeming the time, as my brother-in-law Mike says. I must in every endeavor ask myself, *How will God be glorified?*

HOW WE'RE WIRED

God wired us to work. He was a worker. God's work during creation and his rest on the seventh day leave for us a model by which to pattern our lives and work. Like Adam, all of us have been gifted for a task or even many tasks. But just like God, we need work *and* rest.

The Scriptures tell us God entered into his rest and remains there, waiting for us to join him. And though God's resting place of eternity stands as our hope and even our goal in this life, as well as for the life hereafter, God's rest also provides a model for how we use our leisure time. It's as if we're practicing Sabbath now for the ultimate Sabbath of living with Christ in heaven.[7]

Dr. Gordon Hugenberger, pastor at Park Street Church in Boston, said, "Make sure your celebration of the Lord's Day is a slice of heaven."[8] God did not design the Sabbath to be mindless. He intended us to use it for refreshment. Ask a cyclist what a recovery ride looks like. It helps the body restore itself. You can actually refresh your body while it's in motion. Rest doesn't mean inactivity.

What happens when we turn out the lights, punch the time card, or lay the pen down? "Tim, you're responsible for that time too. I walked with Adam. What do you want to do with me? Let's write another book, or perhaps today we change your suspension."

When we view our leisure and our work not as binary but as a composite whole—both as ways in which to bring glory to God—we find a joy that empowers us with confidence as we use our imaginative agency to infuse life with the blessing of accomplishment. But we veer from this when our leisure time gets hijacked with pointless entertainment and amusement.

***

Matthew Crawford, reflecting on the work of philosopher Albert Borgmann, said we "see that the tension between agency and autonomy can manifest in the meanings of things themselves, or rather in our relationship to them."[9]

Borgmann used the example of an iPod, which he refers to as *a device*, and a guitar, which he refers to as *a thing*. You listen to an iPod, but you must master rules and the physicality demanded in learning to play the guitar. Your relationship to the iPod requires little to no human engagement whereas the guitar can be used as the epicenter of human engagement. I can attest to this fact. I've sat in a room full of bluegrass-playing adults in the hills of Chattanooga, Tennessee, and witnessed firsthand the joy and camaraderie while huddled around instruments, plucking out tunes for hours.

Crawford's reflection on *things* versus *devices* exhorts us to use discernment in what we spend time with and why in our leisure and our work. If we continue down the path of autonomous living, swiping away at our devices and neglecting the more organic, hard things in life, such as learning to play an instrument, growing a garden, or even reading a classic novel, we run the risk of alienating ourselves from the very things that generate significance in our lives—art, music, literature, personal interaction with other human beings, and the rigor of following Christ.

THE BRILLIANCE OF WHOLENESS

Work, for the Christian, looks like a kind of brilliance. It looks like a person using her particular agency to glorify God first and foremost, to serve her fellow human beings, and to contribute to society in a way that promotes the beauty of human flourishing. Aristotle defined *human flourishing* as the innate potential of each individual to live a life of enduring happiness, penetrating wisdom, optimal well-being, and authentic love and compassion.[10]

Don't think that fulfillment escapes God's definition of work for us or that I'm espousing neocommunism. Fulfillment, however, occurs only when we live inside God, within his beam of goodness. We find fulfillment through serving, giving, and experiencing contentment. When our perspective of work changes from what benefits us to how we can glorify God and serve others, fulfillment comes in the most unselfish way possible—through the death of self. When my fingers tingle with grime and I conquer my truck's rear suspension, I can sense God's beam of goodness. I feel his delight through confidence gained, victory won, and a thankful heart.

God's idea of work extends beyond any given task a person

performs each day as a means to make a living. (The whole idea of work related to making a living poses deeper questions about the modern perspective of work that we will not tackle here.) It extends into how we use our leisure time as well.

Our leisure activity should consist of "worship and enjoyment of his creation."[11] In Proverbs, King Solomon describes wisdom in terms of enjoyment and delight. Wisdom says,

> I was the craftsman. . . .
> I was filled with delight day after day, . . .
> rejoicing in his whole world
> and delighting in mankind.[12]

The craftsman metaphor applies to us as well. Even though work is hard and full of toil, it produces delight, for pain can be a source of delight. The marathon runner endures pain for the delight of the finish line; the student hunkers down and endures mental pain and toil for the delight of an earned diploma. In our culture we tend to confuse pleasure with delight. Pleasure, as Volf instructs us, tends toward the sensual, toward experiential satisfaction. Delight originates somewhere outside ourselves, drawing us into the beauty of Christ himself.

**

My father grew up on a farm. His farmer's work ethic carries into both his leisure and his vocation. He works at landscaping the yard, improving the back deck, constructing a retaining wall, or rebuilding my brother's transmission as if God stood next to him saying, "Yes, Whitie, that looks great. What about using some stone here?" or "Perhaps you should check the flywheel in that tranny one more time." No dichotomy exists between the way my father approaches his leisure activities or his day job of shepherding the church as a full-time pastor. He works at both with enjoyment and worship. In both he tends toward discipline, detail, and perseverance.

This solidarity of work as a life ethic looks strange to a secular world that views work as a place to go, a segment of time to give up, or a place to find ultimate personal fulfillment or identity or a means to an end—that end being the accumulation of wealth driven by avarice.

When I danced in the rain, celebrating in jubilant euphoria the suspension sliding into place on my truck, I experienced the same thrill of excitement I receive when I finish a poem or pen the last chapter in a book or think of a new character for my novel. The intent and execution mirror one another, only in different spheres.

Every act as unto the Lord. I work. I play. I work at my play. I dance before the Lord.

Chapter 11

On Imagination

WHY THE STORIES WE HEAR AND TELL MATTER

I am enough of an artist to draw freely upon my imagination. Imagination is more important than knowledge. Knowledge is limited. Imagination encircles the world.
—ALBERT EINSTEIN

After nourishment, shelter and companionship, stories are the thing we need most in the world.
—PHILIP PULLMAN

There are . . . books full of great writing that don't have very good stories. Read sometimes for the story. . . . Don't be like the book-snobs who won't do that. Read sometimes for the words—the language. Don't be like the play-it-safers who won't do that. But when you find a book that has both a good story and good words, treasure that book.
—STEPHEN KING, *HEARTS IN ATLANTIS*

Close your eyes and think about your heart. What sways it? What refreshes it? What invades it? What collapses around it? What strikes fear into it? What moves it? What manipulates it? What lies to it? What controls it?

Author Michael Reeves wrote, "We are made to follow our hearts, to do what we want."[1] The Hebrew word *leb* in the Old Testament means "heart or midst."[2] King Solomon used *leb* when he said, "Guard your heart, for it is the wellspring of life."[3] Our hearts distinguish us from brute beasts. We exist as persons because each of us possesses a heart—the governing center of the physical, intellectual, and psychological. The English words *mind, character*, and *personality* come close to this Hebrew idea of heart.

Some believe when Jesus said, "Love the Lord your God with all your heart and with all your soul, and with all your mind and with all your strength," he was using soul, mind, and strength to describe what it means to love God with your heart. We might read Jesus' words like this: "Love the Lord your God with all your heart; which is your soul, your mind and strength."[4]

Jesus wants us to love him with every aspect of our existence—with all our hearts. When we guard our hearts we guard ourselves against outside influences seeking to make us less of a person. When we follow Christ our hearts experience a renovation. We become new because our hearts—the *all of us*—have become new.

He powers us into newness and baptizes our entire beings when we follow him.[5] But you and I live and breathe in a world of incessant images. Each day we're presented with opportunities to view the horrid and profane, the vulgar and pornographic. We're free to listen to music that takes us to another place, beautiful and true, or to a brooding place, angry and hellish. Through our ears and eyes, sounds and images enter and make their way into our hearts and shape us.

GETTING INSIDE YOUR HEAD

According to the *Oxford Dictionary, imagination* is "the faculty or action of forming new ideas, or images or concepts of external objects not present to the senses." Another, perhaps sharper, definition says *imagination* is "the power of the mind to consider things which are not present to our senses, and to consider that which is not taken to be real."[6]

We can divide our imaginations into two types. The first is our ability to reproduce mental copies of things from our past, and the second is the ability to create. When we say create we don't mean like God creates, from nothing. Rather, we mean the ability to manage images or things into new combinations.[7] Only God creates from nothing. We're just stewards of nature, moving things around in exciting ways—thank you, Aristotle.

It's easy to forget how everything we see and hear passes through the mind's eye and then is either retooled in our reproductive imaginations or put to good use in our productive imaginations. So, whatever passes through this invisible passageway matters. It bends and shapes us as people. It molds our *hearts.*

We don't use our imaginations just when we're finger painting in kindergarten. We use them all the time: to conceptualize a book idea, to wireframe a Web design, to plant a garden, to write a poem, to create a new recipe. The imagination doesn't function as a cognitive tool used only for fantasy—not that there's anything inherently wrong with that (ask Tolkien). It's based in and shaped by reality, it helps us in our work, and it contributes to society at large.

Why do you think presentation software Prezi.com sends e-mails that declare, "Ideas matter"? Because Prezi.com understands the imagination fuels the production of cultural goods ranging from nonfiction books to documentaries, from works of fiction and movies to brand strategy, from forming social nonprofits to evangelism, and the list continues.

We also employ our imaginations in our relationship with God. Remember, imagination is a tool for seeing what is there when our senses fail.[8] God exists as our everyday reality, and we rev up our imaginations to communicate with and worship him. Timothy Williamson, *New York Times* columnist and Oxford professor in logic, said, "Imagining turns out to be much more reality-directed than the stereotype implies. . . . The imagination is not just a random idea generator."[9]

You might say the imagination acts as a portal, connecting the heart to the world of the invisible, and translating the world of the visible into mind fuel for future imaginative agency.

THE POINT OF STORY

Story, perhaps more than anything else, engages the imagination. Like a baseball hitting a glove, stories are meant to live inside one another. Jesus used stories to teach practical truth about his coming kingdom, about everyday wisdom, about God, and about himself. The gospel writer Matthew stated, "All these things Jesus said to the crowds in parables; indeed, he said nothing to them without a parable."[10] Jesus' parables—simple stories used to illustrate a moral—struck his listeners' hearts with truth, influencing them in the positive and the negative. The mustard seed parable tells us how pure faith contains great power; it can move mountains, a positive message. The story of the talents reminds us we're responsible for the things and abilities with which God has entrusted us; the moral is both positive and cautionary.

Jesus told stories because story is a common language of the people. When you connect through the heart, the head will follow. *Stories are powerful, yet simple, tools we use and the world uses to teach and to shape our hearts.* If you agree, you understand how important it is to steward our use of stories as well as to manage the kinds of stories we allow to shape our hearts.

Plato thought stories were the best tools for training children in morality. Stories make us feel and even produce affections toward certain moral judgments, developing moral virtues "such as honesty, courage, diligence, generosity and responsibility."[11] But in the same way stories connect and teach us in positive ways, they can work in negative ways. We, as a culture, riddle our stories with elements of the obscene, the vulgar, the grotesque, and the hypersexualized. We consume hours and hours of media saturated with this hideous content and scratch our heads at the divorce rate, the bloated fatherlessness, and the outright moral decay of the Millennial generation. "The U.S. has created a moral system based on convenience, feelings, and selfishness."[12]

The stories with which we engage infiltrate our hearts and shape society into various normative behaviors. Looks like Plato was right—whether moral or amoral, these stories teach us something, and we adopt it for ourselves and for all society. So we must ask ourselves, *What stories are we watching, listening to, and participating in?*

Have our hearts feasted so much on cynicism, despair, and silly vulgarity that we have no taste for whimsy and hope? Stories abound in all media channels, but just because they exist does not mean we should consume them without thinking about their origin or intent. Since when did Christians relegate their imaginations and ultimately their hearts to something or someone other than God himself—or the things of God, things of truth, things of goodness, things of beauty?

OUR STORY, THE ENDURING MYTH OF LIGHT

How do we break through the shadow-media invading our imaginations through bland stories, toxic images, and dim views of humanity? We infuse our imaginations with the glory and spellbinding goodness of the gospel—a holy incantation of imagination, turning darkness to light.

In the first place, we should recognize the power and beauty of the Christian faith. It is a faith expression that should read true, written out in beautiful script on our lives. It's a story of wonder, pain, and victory. The world should read the myth of Christianity, compare it to other religious stories, and find God's narrative alive. We use *myth* here not in the secondary meaning held in popular discourse as a "widely held but false belief." Instead, we use *myth* to describe the story of God chasing us, through Christ, as a narrative invoking awe and wonder. For myth is but a story told to invoke amazement and surprise, to infuse a person with a sense of otherness. A myth "weaves together truth and meaning, engaging with both our reason and imagination."[14]

Our hearts resonate with truth and meaning, remember? We were meant to run on soulish things.

In the second place, we employ our imaginations to produce actual stories. We feel the irony of this statement even as we put forth our ideas in a nonfiction book. But we're given to elevating those among the family of God who are producing works of story set forth in fiction, film, theater, poetry, music, dance, and other forms of what many consider the beautiful arts. These forms of art thrive on storytelling. We are also trying our hands at storytelling through our works.

It doesn't matter whether we are the storytellers, the gatekeepers to story distribution, or the consumers of stories. All of us should consider ourselves stewards of imagination. We should tell our own stories of hope, grace, forgiveness, and salvation while we champion people within the arts by encouraging them and distributing their work into the greater culture.

In the third place, we should see ourselves as heart guardians. To do so we must realize the inherent nature of discernment within our aesthetic decisions. So much of taste in film and music and other visual and auditory art rests on personal preference. But what guides our preferences?

Philosopher Peter Kreeft said, "Moral duty is not duty for duty's sake. It leads yonder, taking beauty and joy with it." So we're not saying we should put on our sour faces and become moralists. On the contrary, we think we should become beauty seekers, for "beauty is not the absolute but points beyond itself."[15] That place beyond is God. And when he becomes our *first thing,* as Kreeft puts it, our filters for beautiful stories will be refined. We will find the more we begin with God, the more nourished our hearts will become. The rest fixes itself.

Chapter 12

To Kill a Mockingmouse or Something for Wives to Pass to Their Husbands

REEXAMINING MANLINESS

If you can fill the unforgiving minute
With sixty seconds' worth of distance run,
Yours is the Earth and everything that's in it,
And—which is more—you'll be a Man, my son!
—RUDYARD KIPLING, "IF"

A man must at times be hard as nails: willing to face up to the truth
about himself and about the woman he loves, refusing compromise
when compromise is wrong. But he must also be tender. No weapon
will breach the armor of a woman's resentment like tenderness.

—ELISABETH ELLIOT, *MARK OF A MAN*

We [modern society] make men without chests and expect of them
virtue and enterprise. We laugh at honour and are shocked to find
traitors in our midst. We castrate and bid the geldings be fruitful.

—C. S. LEWIS, *THE ABOLITION OF MAN*

Both of us consider ourselves manly men. Tim works on his own vehicle, and Jason wears flannel and grows a mean-looking winter beard. Both of us like strong, dark coffee, wear shoes made from leather, and buy Levi's jeans. On Saturdays we lace up our work boots and don our sweat-stained hats as we prepare to toil in our yards like little Wendell Berrys, content to cultivate our plot of sub-urban soil. On Sundays we ignore our doctors' cholesterol warnings and eat a cornucopia of sodium-filled snacks while watching other manly men run around carrying a ball made of pigskin.

We are men.

But all this modern-day testosterone plumage was tested one autumn day. Our families were enjoying the fall foliage during our annual trip to the Appalachian Mountains. The kids rolled down the hills screaming and took turns with the daddies on the four-wheeler. But inside the cabin, one of the children found a dead mouse sitting like an ornament in a decorative seasonal basket. The threat of the mighty creature's presence haunted us throughout the day as we wondered when one of his nondead friends might make the rounds.

Later that evening Tim found Fievel's friend alive and well.

As we sat by the fire with our wives playing Uno with the older boys, enjoying the quiet after the little kids went to bed, Tim saw something scurry under the door of his two-year-old daughter's room.

"Did you see that?"

"What? What did you see?"

The quiet game of Uno turned into Defcon 1. Tim asked for cover, darted into the room, flipped on the light, and rescued his daughter. Jason's son spotted the critter behind a bureau and shouted,

"There he is!" Jason snatched a broom from the closet and leaped onto the bed for an aerial view. The hunt was on!

The mouse, sensing Jason's presence, scampered under the door to the adjacent bathroom. Jason's wife, Heather, eyed the vermin behind the toilet.

With Skywalkeresque broom skills, Jason poked the bristled saber in the direction of Heather's pointing finger. The mouse somersaulted out; stunned and disoriented, he limped back behind the bureau in the bedroom. Tim grabbed a walking stick near the front door and urged the mouse out once more. Jason waited high on his bedside perch, poised to pounce.

The two men were too much for the furry little one. The mouse scuttled out, and Jason jabbed it with the broom.

The hunt was over.

The mouse, dead.

MEN OR MICE?

Does killing a mouse make us real men? Who are we as men in this metrosexualized world of buffoonery-sitcom males and designer-flannel wannabes? What does a real God-made man look like?

The mouse incident incited a larger discussion between Tim and me. We revisited some of the numbers surrounding an issue that many refer to as "fatherlessness." We like to call it "manlessness." Our nation's divorce rate is between 40 and 50 percent. Forty-one percent of all births in the United States occur outside marriage. Nearly 50 percent of all men in this country father at least one child outside marriage.[1]

A hundred years ago fatherlessness was a result of paternal death. Men today are not physically dying as much as they're choosing to live socially dead. When you consider a child born outside marriage spends only six months of his entire childhood living with his father, it's not so farfetched to view manhood through an Ashton Kutcheresque lens.

"He just came up and kissed me," twenty-two-year-old Sara Leal told *US Weekly*. "He lost his towel and I took my robe off."[2] The article chronicles the now famous one-night stand that contributed to the ruin of a marriage and the tabloid stardom of a young woman. It also profiles a man who has now become a role model for all twenty- and thirty-something wannabe playboys: Ashton Kutcher. For most men, this real-life scenario happens only in the movies. A film like *The Hangover* propagates the Hollywood gospel that says manhood equals debauchery, laziness, and irresponsibility. If you believe what you see on the big screen and in Mr. Kutcher's hot tub, manhood looks like being a slightly better dressed teenager.

The mouse killing was a beginning point, a comical ruse to awaken thoughts of what manliness looks like. Films and sitcoms cast manhood as a mindless endeavor defined by what we can get from society: *money and power.* We are encouraged to chart a narcissistic course through life, racking up notches on our bedposts, dollars in our bank accounts, and toys in our garages. Manhood looks like a trophy we win, a card we carry, an image we curate, rather than the relationships we cultivate.

Men, we are men. We are strong yet tender, bold yet caring, stern yet loving. We are not the one-dimensional sitcom versions of ourselves. We've allowed the world to dim our brilliance. We want to reignite it.

THE WEIGHT IS A GIFT

My (Jason's) wife considered adoption first. She nudged me along in a two-year conversation centered on why our family should adopt. My counterargument was always the same: We already have two amazing boys and life's good. Why rock the boat? Let's not overdo the blessings. Two kids are plenty. Our hands are full. More kids? What are you thinking?

I remember when I finally agreed to attend the mandatory information meeting on adoption. At the time we were considering international adoption, and my attitude was less than excited. We drove the thirty minutes to town and walked into a large room with gray metal folding chairs and drab-gray carpet. Nothing says hope like the buzz of fluorescent lighting.

We found seats and started reviewing the handout, a four-page Excel spreadsheet. Each row represented a country open to adoption, and each column gave a piece of information such as wait time or price or necessary travel. In what amounted to possibly the most boring hour of my life, the instructor read through the spreadsheet row by row and column by column. Really, this is your plan to convince people to adopt? Read them a spreadsheet?

As I sat there redesigning the experience in my head, the thought crept in that adoption would be great if it didn't take thousands of dollars, tons of forms to fill out, multiple visits to a foreign country, and complex legal work. Sometime between counting ceiling tiles and thinking of the arduous road of red tape that lay before us, a voice popped into my head: *If you weren't such a selfish jerk, imagine how rich your life would be.*

I am selfish. Even that thought was selfish. *My life would be richer if I weren't selfish.* I am so selfish that even my thoughts about not being selfish somehow point out the benefit to me.

***

When Ethan, our first, was born, I was a mess. I had no idea what we were doing. I remember the nurse looking at me after his birth. "Okay, Dad, time for a diaper change."

I stood there and looked at her and smiled, *Okay, well, let me know when you are done so I can get back to looking at him.*

She smiled back. "No, *you* are changing the diaper."

Whoa, I am a dad now, I thought.

Ethan was my responsibility, and life wasn't just about me anymore; it was about him. That responsibility weighs more than anything else in the world—knowing that someone trusts you to be there for him and letting him down could mean damaging him forever. It's so important that entire professions exist to help adults with bad dads. But as Nada Surf once said, "The weight is a gift."[3]

***

As I sat thinking to the hum of the fluorescent lights, I realized I wasn't against adoption or against more kids. No, I was against inconveniencing myself. I was against taking more time away from *me.* I was fearful I wouldn't build my work in the way I wanted, or I wouldn't have enough money to buy new boots or a new gizmo. I realized, for the first time, the beautiful gift of responsibility. And something rose inside me and took hold of the weight. It hurt a bit, but pride usually does when it's trounced by love.

That night at the adoption meeting affected how I viewed the next year and our two eventual domestic adoptions. Adoption wasn't about me; it was about a birth mother brave enough—loving enough—to make a hard choice. All I needed to do was shut up and follow the clear path that God had paved for me.

With each kid the weighty gift looks a shade different. With Ethan, it was figuring out what in the world we were doing; and with Christian, it was adjusting to two. Naomi was a burst of brilliance as we entered and navigated the adoption process. With Eliana, it was about how to manage all four.

But responsibility is much more than what each child represents to me. Responsibility weighs as much as life itself: the life of each of my children. And if every day I can get past *me,* I can embrace them—their formation, their passions, their quirks, their exasperating and beautifully holy lives.

BE A MAN FOR YOUR KIDS

Being a responsible man is a serious endeavor. It influences how our daughters view their future husbands and how our sons treat their wives and their sons. Historically men perform manly things together, living life in close proximity to one another. Society thinks it's certain things we do—killing a mouse, watching NASCAR, and drinking beer—that make us men. These perceived masculine activities miss the point. It's not what men and their kids do necessarily; it's their togetherness. It's being there.

Sometimes I take one of my sons to Taco Mac, the local sports bar. We gawk at the one hundred TVs hanging around us, blasting the game of the day. My son talks my ear off, reciting every stat of every New York Giants player from every game of the last two years. We talk about soccer practice and school and tell funny stories. Then more about the Giants.

After the chips and queso and his third root beer, I push him toward something different. Here our activity of going to Taco Mac shifts from being something we do to our experiencing togetherness.

"What are you thankful for?" I ask.

"Um," he pauses. "I don't know."

"Well, think about it for a second."

"Um. That the Giants won the Super Bowl."

"Yeah, that's good," I reply. "What about something else?"

"I guess I am thankful for Eliana," he says.

"Yes, God has blessed you with a beautiful sister." I smile. "Has God shown you anything new or neat lately?"

"I guess to be thankful for lots of stuff," he answers.

There, we did it. We had a conversation. When we head to Taco Mac, sure, it's about going somewhere together, but when we connect through meaningful conversation, our encounter elevates to another level. By initiating our conversation, I model how he should act around other men as he grows older. I want him to know that it's okay to ask his buddies about thankfulness. I want him to probe and be unafraid to ask his friends if God has shown them anything neat. Why not?

Other times, we find ourselves working through hard issues. One night, my son lashed out at the rest of the family. I dragged him into the car and drove. For forty-five minutes we drove nowhere and got nowhere in our conversation. The two of us sat somewhere between silence and frustration.

I didn't know what to do so I started praying with him: "Heavenly Father, help our conversation, and give Mom and Dad wisdom so we know how to help." During the prayer, though, something happened. I started to confess things to God, no longer caring that my son could hear me. I confessed the brokenness of our family over the last couple of months. I confessed my unkindness to Heather. I confessed my uncertainty about the darkness I felt lingering over our family and house. I turned from crying out to God for help to crying *with* God about our family. I pulled the car over to the shoulder and wept.

My son sat there, sniffling, tears squeezing their way out of his eyes.

"Sorry," he whispered.

"Look, buddy, this isn't your fault," I replied. "There is something bigger happening here. We're not acting the way God wants our family to act. This isn't all about you and tonight. God wants our family to reflect his love, and right now we don't. We need to fix that."

"I'm sorry, Dad," he repeated. It was a sincere gesture from a ten-year-old boy who didn't know what to say to his crying father.

"I know, buddy, and it's okay. Things will work out."

We spent the next couple of minutes on the side of the road talking about how God wants our family to act toward one another. We talked about grace and love and forgiveness and God's amazing love for us.

I explained how sometimes grown-ups cry too, so he didn't need to feel freaked out. I told him all of us need the help of our heavenly Father. I affirmed how the world looks like an ugly place sometimes but explained how even the ugliest of uglies cannot keep God from working his plan for our family. I told him I loved him and wrapped my arms around him, blanketing him.

I don't know if he understood it all, but I think he accepted it. It gave him freedom to be scared, to show his emotions, to cry out, and to talk about it all with me.

***

A relational exchange occurs when I talk with my son about football and thankfulness at Taco Mac, when I cry with them over the unknown. In the Christian world we call this "discipleship." The activity works only as the beginning point, the platform from which to press deeper into each other's life.

Manhood rises from the fires of testing ourselves against the men who mean the most to us. My children run up against me, testing how tender my soul feels, how deep my joy runs, and how firm my love stands. In daily events I model for them what a man looks like and how he acts. In our togetherness we bond, and with time I see the little boy who snuggled in the crook of my arm sprout into a man.

BE A MAN FOR YOUR WIFE

When I (Tim) talk to Chris, my wife, I am doing more than transmitting information from me to her. Little ears perk up from behind the couch and catch every word. My words carry weight. One day, my daughters will find them acceptable or unacceptable from the boys they date and the men they marry. "My dad never talked like that to me," they will say. At least that's what I want them to say.

When I talk to Chris, I model for them what a loving husband sounds like. Sometimes the sound stings.

When I think about the diminishing of God's intended brilliance in men—as fathers, husbands, workers, adventurers, lovers, life-poets, and the sacrificial lambs for their wives—I cannot hold back the shame. How I've blown it again and again.

I remember being alone in the truck one day during my second year of marriage and wondering out loud, "What am I doing?" I doubted my decision to marry. I doubted my ability to be what I already thought I was: a good man. I was arrogant and delusional. If beauty existed in marriage, I couldn't find it.

When things were good, early on, they were great. When they were bad, they were downright ugly.

But now, Chris and I have waded into new waters—knee deep in our twelfth year. We continue to chase dreams: dreams to raise our girls in a God-honoring fashion, dreams to pursue a PhD in England, dreams to write books, dreams to find an old farm out west and make a place for others to come and learn, question, and love God deeper. Through it all, Chris and I must continue to communicate. It's the glue to our marriage.

I'm a talker. My words, however, do not always bring joy. Often, because I can wield them with pith and thrift, I bash and claw over those I love most. Many, if not all, of us can relate to family discord on Sunday mornings. I know I'm guilty. I've even used expletives on the way to church, followed by a hollow attempt to sing a praise song once in my seat in the sanctuary. I am the chief of sinners and hypocrites.

Each Sunday our church sets the Communion table and then offers the wafer and the wine. We're given time to reflect on the message and encouraged to search our souls for unconfessed wrongs.

God has taught me the power of confession through this time of Communion and reflection. I may bash and claw, but I know that I do it. I'm aware. After awareness I must climb my steepest relational hill: confession. It must move from my lips first. It must pull in my love and whisper to her. This is the hardest thing a man can do.

When I hear the music play, soft and ethereal in the background, I run to God. I no longer sit in my church chair but am transported to the foot of the cross. And there he sits mangled and disfigured. He gasps for breath. The sky looks like a dark vise, pressing the life out of him.

And there hangs the thief. I can hear him *confess*.

I love how Billy Graham frames Golgotha. He says Christ became every sinner on the day he died. I look at Christ again and see someone else—a prostitute, a murderer, a rapist, an adulterer, a molester, a liar, a cheater, and an everyman sinner. No matter how heinous the sin, he took it *all*.

He who knew no sin *became* sin itself.

There I sit at church and atop Golgotha. I see him become my sin, and then the confession comes out of me like the water from his side. I pull Chris close and whisper, "Can we pray?"

She approves and grabs my hand. I pray and thank Christ for her and the girls. In her ear I ask God to forgive my words and my unkindness. She hears me ask for *his* strength as I struggle to follow *his* way. We don't always need to confess during Communion—we do have good weeks. We even have great weeks. But the hard weeks, the weeks in which my words crash into Chris and the kids, I know of nothing I'd rather do than run to Golgotha.

* * *

One professor in graduate school told me an eye-opening story about his mentor. The mentor was offered his dream job at his dream school. But his wife didn't feel they should move. She wanted to stay. The common response from many of my evangelical friends when I asked them how they'd react was, "Well, she should follow her husband."

But the opposite is true.

My professor told how his mentor chose, instead of pulling the family-leader card, to nail himself to the tree and die. Paul exhorts all men to die in service to their wives.[4] Loving my wife and children the way Christ loves the church sounds like beautiful talk. Sometimes I feel a burst of manliness quake inside me. But if I stop and step back, I find it's not manliness at all. It's a pitch of lies pushing up through my old flesh: *You're the man, make them listen, make them follow, make them, make them.*

I'm far away from the doubting and confused Tim in the pickup.

My girls inspire me. They breathe a life into me I never thought existed. Their love beckons my true manliness. It's not in the making. It's in the quieting. It's in the caressing. It's in the playing. It's in the wooing. It's in the singing. It's in the storytelling. It's in the whispering—the whispering upon Golgotha while holding Chris's hand: "I'm sorry. Please forgive me."

PROVERBS 32

It's easy to cuss and grunt and build a fire. Cavemen did all that. Despite popular belief, doing these things doesn't make us men. We think it's time to redefine manhood or, better yet, reset it. So, we've done what John the Beloved said we shouldn't do: we've added a chapter to the Bible. We don't think John would mind, though. In fact, we think John would approve of this exercise—using holy Writ as our template to write down a major reminder of what a man should be.

If a Proverbs 32 man existed, we think he would look this:

A PROVERBS 32 MAN

A good man is hard to find. His wife trusts him without reserve and never has reason to regret it.

Never spiteful, he showers blessings all life long.

He enjoys his work, pursuing a meaningful vocational existence, and seeks God's purpose.

He doesn't waste time on temporal pleasures such as *Modern Warfare* or *Breaking Bad*. Instead, he gets his lazy backside up and studies the Word and prays for his family before he organizes his day.

He doesn't squander his money on frivolous things like gambling or stupid gadgets. Rather, he invests in things that last: his children's education, something beautiful for his wife, and a thoughtful retirement plan.

He senses the worth of his work but knows when it's time to go home and see his family.

He doesn't slough off home repairs and at least tries to fix the garbage disposal; he mows his own yard, modeling what it means to find the joy in agency.

He's quick to assist anyone in need and reaches out to help the poor.

He doesn't worry about his family when it snows. He's prepared—he's done his due diligence.

He's greatly respected when he deliberates with community leaders.

He's not afraid to get his hands dirty. He tries to change his brake pads and enjoys whittling wood.

He looks sharp and dresses appropriately for the occasion without relinquishing who he is at his core.

When he speaks he does so with language that uplifts. He doesn't use coarse talk because he thinks it's cool. He employs discernment and always speaks with kindness.

He's the head of his household but rules with deft discernment—understanding the value that Christ rules it all and the importance of what it means for his wife to be co-equal.

His children respect and bless him; his wife joins in with words of praise: "Many men have done wonderful things, but you've outclassed them all!"

He handles influence, which can mislead, and understands that power soon fades.

The man to be admired and praised is the man who lives in the fear of God.

Chapter 13

The Sound and the Fury

ON WHAT'S NEEDED TO ENDURE
THE SEASONS OF LIFE

Even when we are weighed down with troubles, it is for your comfort and salvation! For when we ourselves are comforted, we will certainly comfort you.
—PAUL THE APOSTLE

To hold on to the plow while wiping our tears—this is Christianity.
—WATCHMAN NEE

"Love is recognizable only by love."
—SOREN KIERKEGAARD, *WORKS OF LOVE*

I (Tim) sat motionless on the floor. A pale light filled the room and, for a moment, kept the shadows at bay. I faced the lone window and stared above the evergreen treetops. Light snow flecked against their dark silhouettes. I shoved open the old window and listened. I heard the hollow sound of wind passing through the evergreen groves and barren oaks standing in the valley just behind the house. The green giants moaned, then creaked. Then all was calm. The winter air began to fill the room, but I didn't care.

I kept listening for more sounds; I kept staring at the fading winter day. The pale light turned gray and finally gave in to the shadows pushing it across the floor. Winter's night had come.

I could hear post-Christmas bustle and banter downstairs. Life moved and chattered among my Johnstown family, my wife's mother and father and aunts and uncles and cousins laughed and ate, while the dead time of snow and cold quietly put the world to sleep outside. I was caught between two worlds—the living voices below and the dead voices outside. And in my in-between world of observation and silence, tears welled as I wrote frantically in my journal. I wrote of my love for my new family. I wrote of my love for my own family enduring the Christmas cold in Lancaster, Pennsylvania, on this night of nights.

In those quiet moments we so easily break and our souls reach to climb inside those we love. I wrote and wept for love.

It extends farther than you think, the reach of your love, the reach of your life. It reaches high. It is taller than trees. It has been planted and cared for and we have grown so close for so long I forget when we were ever apart. I feel as though our souls were waiting for life together in some cosmic paradise, a waiting room for the souls of the world, the threshold of eternity.

How the everlasting stretches out in my mind. What a wonderful paradox: eternity placed in us by the Maker yet lost in the depths of our spirits. Perhaps we strive for the love that comes out of eternity, the everlasting knowing from one end of the stars to the other. We search for ways to express it and hold on to the thoughts of love like the barren trees of winter—these barren trees in front of me, standing next to the green giants—cling to the passing wind.

They reach to cling but do not grasp. But in the reaching a mystery is created. And when on a night like tonight, we see the trees and hear them in the valley, that mystery climbs up our spines and pulls us close. We run to capture it—as I do now—on paper or canvas or something, or some way we cannot explain, in a song perhaps. Oh, the mystery of wind passing through barren trees! Oh, the mystery of this eternal love I so desperately reach to hold. Our lives fill with moments of perpetual grasping of this love.

But the limbs of the trees capture something, don't they? They capture the sway produced by the wintry gales; they seize the whistling in the upper branches. Their grand gestures in the waning half light whisper, "Though death is all around and snow blankets the mountains, life still comes. It moves in and through us."

The barren trees and evergreen grove stand at attention, waiting out this nothing time of winter for the grand reawakening of spring. And this is what captures us—what stirs our hearts with wonder. Their quiet song of creaks and moans and whistles beckons to the anticipation of the great push.

So it is with my love for my family and friends. So many times sitting in a room not saying a word causes a deep peace and a longing for more of the same. That is what love is, being in the same room with someone and not needing to say a word—the Spirit wind moving among us, causing our souls to moan in quiet undulating prayer.

Silence is the whisper language of love, and I am whispering to you all—you the reader, you my family, you my friends—at this time. In the quiet stillness of winter, in this room dimming with the sun, I am speaking to you in whispers of silence. I am connecting with your spirits through a cosmic portal, whispering like the trees in the wind, like the sway in the upper branches. How I reach for you all, like these trees reach. Our love is taller than trees.

THE DYNAMIC FURY OF LIFE

Give me each season in all its dynamic fury. Give me the shadow flag of winter. Give me the faerie sunshine of spring. Give me the dancing rainbows of summer. Give me the turbulence of autumn. In it all the cycle of life reveals itself to us. In spring the seeds go into the ground, the rains water, and the sun warms. Then we harvest the seeds that have grown from the cold, dark soil into the gourds and corn of autumn. Finally, the death-like season of winter covers the living in its quilt of quiet.

The magic of birth, of a child entering a hardened world, and of the ensuing growth into adolescence and then adulthood dazzle me. There is also the magic of beauty coming forth from age. Like the mature trees in the valley, human aging brings quiet confidence. Storytelling comes forth from my mother's eyes. It is deep in my father's

eyes as well. It is a story of struggle, toil, and hurt, of love, joy, and celebration. The echoes of prayers ring through their lives like sleigh bells
on a winter's night, ushering in contentment, granting peace.

We push through the seasons of life like the crocus, out of dirt,
into glory, into death. All the while we collect the sunlight of life
in the form of experience and knowledge. The longer we live, the
more we understand, the more we do, the more we hurt. Each crocus brings its own unique glory. Each dainty plant adds its beauty to
the whole of the landscape until we gasp, half choking on the magnificence. Without individual crocuses the beauty in the landscape
stands incomplete.

And so it is with you and me. The Maker purposed the world
with you in mind. I stand incomplete without you. Your beauty
adds much to my pushing, dirty life. Like when you struggled in
the autumn storm, nearly dying from the flood. You yearned for the
quiet of winter, and now I clamor to escape this winter—the nothing
and solemnity. Your struggle and bruises encourage me as I cycle
through the seasons of life.

Life carries on like the seasons. We grow and endure. We flour-
ish and suffer. We increase and fall away. We harvest and germinate.
But what is the point?

To love and be loved.

The dynamic of suffering and victory throws us into the grand
story arc of God. We love in order to see his face. We suffer in order
to *be* his face to loved ones.

But the seasons show us the strength of this love. This love deter-
mines the work of a thing. It tills the soil and sloshes through the
rain. It prepares the fields and wakes early to tend and cultivate.

It rejoices in growth but does not lose sight of the harvest. It cares for the land surrounding the crop. It readies the reservoir in case of drought. It rests.

It suffers the length of the dark autumn mornings in harvest. It does not rest until the barns burgeon. It looks to future need. It stares at winter and does not flinch. Love never fails.

THE SPIRIT OF COMFORT

Where are you in the fury? Wasting away in your solitary winter? Scrambling through a summer drought? How far does your love extend to those closest to you?

In this life you and I will suffer. But we will also experience the joy of harvest. Like the seasons, life changes. But our seasons require us to look outward. If we fail in this, we will wither. Kept to ourselves, the seasons become nothing more than the constant outward wasting away of life.

But the cycle continues. Always a new seed finds its way into the ground. Always there stands another who needs to know how to navigate the waiting of summer, the cutting of autumn, and the death of winter. Our experiences are the water to comfort others.

Paul reminds his readers that God comforts us so that we can be a comfort to others.[1] The dynamic of our lives directly affects and possesses the power to encourage someone else. This is why we can't allow life to force us into ourselves. God's comfort overflows into our lives; our comfort should overflow into others' lives. What joy to share in sufferings *and* comfort!

LOVE, OUR SHINING VEIL

When I shut the window, the warmth of the house returned. I shook off the cold and continued to write. I could taste the quiet and the lingering love within it. From down below the Christmas conversation ebbed on with exclamation points of laughter—the smell of coffee etching the memory into permanence. When I closed my eyes I saw my family, three hours to the east, lost in laughter and coffee and cherry surprise.

It was winter, and all of us huddled close to our roots. We fed our depths with one another as the snow fell, as the wind blew, as winter carried on. Our love reaches taller than trees, but it begins in the roots. It continues in the shared experiences and the fury of life. It galvanizes in the endurance needed to make it just one more day. It is our shining veil, like the sunlight on March soil.

How I need you all to make it through.

In our hearts we all feel the sentence of death. But who accuses? Not the Comforter, not me. I am reaching for you even through the opacity of words written on paper. I am reaching for you like these barren trees reach for the wind. And what I grasp is not the wind itself but the sound and the fury.

Chapter 14

Oak Shadows and Autumn Sun

WE ARE BRILLIANCE MAKERS AND SHADOW CHASERS

But when thou dost anneal in glass thy story,

Making thy life to shine within

The holy preachers, then the light and glory

More reverend grows, and more doth win;

Which else shows waterish, bleak, and thin.

—GEORGE HERBERT, "THE WINDOW"

You'll miss the best things if you keep your eyes shut.

—DR. SEUSS, *I CAN READ WITH MY EYES SHUT!*

Afflictions are but the shadow of God's wings.

—GEORGE MACDONALD

When I (Tim) was in the fifth grade, my teacher, Mrs. Wilson, required the class to memorize Robert Frost's poem "Stopping by Woods on a Snowy Evening." She might as well have assigned us Homer's *Iliad*. That's how long it felt to work through. The rigor of committing this poem to memory, however, burned certain images into my young psyche—images I still remember with fondness: a quiet wood filling up with snow; a distant village, which I was about to enter; the desire to stay while feeling the push to move on—not so much an image but a strong feeling.

As I worked through each stanza, the poem took shape in my mind and arrested my ten-year-old heart. I loved those woods. I wanted to go there and often would in daydreams. I felt those woods were really mine, even though they belonged to someone in the village.

I didn't realize it at the time, but Frost was working telepathy on me. Stephen King says all writers are masters of telepathy in that they can make you think what they are thinking—they empty their brains on the paper and you read their words, thus thinking the thoughts of another person. Telepathy![1] I believe King is correct, for I was thinking Frost's thoughts and experiencing *something* that felt real but existed only in words written on Mrs. Wilson's chalkboard.

That *something* experienced I now understand as beauty.

"Every time a poem is written," said Frost in one of his lectures, "every time a short story is written, it is written not by cunning, but by belief. The beauty, the *something*, the little charm of the thing to be, is more felt than known."[2] I *felt* the charm of the woods on a snowy evening and have been feeling it ever since in the way the wind puffs the white curtains in my study on a breezy autumn day, in the way a song touches me, in the way my daughters play in mud puddles, giggling.

When we buried my grandma five years ago, we laid her beside my grandpa in a quiet cemetery plot nestled on the side of a Johnstown, Pennsylvania, mountain. A small chapel with red doors stood watch as the barren winter trees whistled their requiem. I remember that day like I remember the Frost poem, in feelings stirred by images burned into my imagination. The event was solemn and sad, like a poem can be, but that dark moment at the graveside produced its own charm within me. I remember Grandma in all her quirky good cheer—her quick wit and never-failing love for professional football. I remember how she always wanted me to cut my hair so she could see my "pretty blue eyes."

As the memory of Grandma passes, sadness sweeps into me. It's odd how sadness can rise from a memory and then turn to nostalgia. I can hear Grandma talking football with me all over again just like I feel Frost's snowy woods all over again.

What Frost refers to as "the beauty, the *something*, the little charm," I call "transcendence." But unlike Frost, I believe the charm of transcendence can be felt *and* known. It is the known part of tran-scendence that allows me to call the graveside time beautiful. This *known* part is God.

It is the known part that pushes us toward belief—belief that no matter how dark today seems, the sun will rise tomorrow. To *believe* is no small task. When we believe something we give intellectual assent to the truth of something or someone. Our actions then typically align with our beliefs.

Many believe the world is wasting away, and they act accordingly. Many believe life to be pointless, and their lifestyle shows it. In recent years many Americans believe their economic future will never recover. It's easy to see things and then form our beliefs around them or the by-products of them. But what if a person believed in something invisible? What if a person could look at a pending economic crisis and see hope? What does it take to see the invisible?

Isaiah, the Old Testament prophet, wrote that the earth will one day wear out like a garment.[3] John the Beloved said that "the world is passing away along with its desires."[4] But this is where the *known* part of beauty takes over—where a belief in an invisible God can make all the difference.

When I envision what John the Beloved is saying here, I picture the world existing in the waning shadows of an autumn afternoon. Shadows lengthen as the sun falls and passes over the landscape. And yet at the same time the sunlight takes on an otherworldly look, beaming with a scintillating crispness that can lure you away from whatever you're doing and out into a field, chasing the fading autumn brilliance.

So, what you have in the phenomenon of the autumn sunset is a simultaneous dying of the day along with the richest and most alive light of the day. The clear and unfiltered autumn light reveals, in a metaphorical way, a mysterious message from God that illumines and quickens even when the darkest shadows of life run deep on the landscape of our souls.

That message?

It is the act of chasing brilliance that keeps hope alive within our hearts. And that chasing act produces an expectation of belief—that though the shadows lengthen and at times overwhelm, the brilliance is not far away.

You and I know that "we live in the shadowlands."[5] But we know this only because we see brilliance pushing across the landscape. For where there is shadow, there is light, and where there is light, hope shines.

When I watch my girls play in the waning autumn sun, jumping in and out of the oak shadows strewn across the backyard, I think of God's mysterious message, his good news. This news swept through small villages and kings' palaces in the first century. It was a proclamation: *the long-awaited Messiah had come; his kingdom was now and also to come.* It provided us with redemption from our sinful rebellion and offered us a new way to live. And that is the beautiful mystery of it all—it is the man Christ Jesus; it is what he provided for each one of us.

As I reflect on it, I see that each of us has the ability to move from shadow to light without any permanent soul damage once our gaze is fixed on Christ, once we step into a relationship with him. My daughters will lay their heads down when the sun retires for the evening. And yet morning comes again; with it my girls will rise to the brilliance spilling into their window. We, too, will rise tomorrow to the brilliance with another opportunity to step from our shadows and into the brilliance, the beauty, the charm of the gospel, the charm and transcendence of Christ himself.

The world is passing. And yet this mysterious message, this good news, gives us the opportunity to rise into its brilliance and seize it forever. We wait as the shadows pass, abiding, waiting on the hope that comes from the brilliance. Waiting on God and the brilliance of Christ.

Discussion Guide

We read to know that we are not alone.

—WILLIAM NICHOLSON

As you read through the book we hope you will reflect on what you're learning. Maybe you'll flip these pages with a friend, a spouse, a daughter, or a son. We encourage this group reading and the conversations that will follow. Even if your friends don't read the book, talk to them about it anyway. Who knows where the conversation may lead?

And if you're learning a lot, it's okay to annoy your friends with it a little. Like when you discover a new band and can't stop talking about the latest album. You never know whom you may encourage with your thoughts.

To facilitate that discussion we outlined ideas that emerged while we wrote the book. We then structured those thoughts in a way suitable for, say, your quiet time or small-group conversations. Each chapter is presented in two sections: "Reflection" and "Discussion."

The reflection is something for you to think about while driving or taking a shower or sitting with your morning coffee. Use these times to carve out mental space to process what you are reading. No need to rush through the book. We aren't offering prizes for the fastest read, so let your thoughts simmer.

Once you have reflected and prayed, talk to someone about what God is revealing. The discussion questions push toward that. And, hey, don't be a robot. These are conversation kick-starters, but feel free to talk about whatever you want. The point is to talk, not follow the guide. The more time you reflect, the richer the discussion.

Okay, time to dig in.

Prologue: Discussion

The Brilliance of Home

REFLECTION

We looked for a time in our schedules that allowed us to sneak away for just a day and finish the book. This wasn't easy since we were both selling our homes and dealing with all the business that entails. Jason's work at his day job piled up, and Tim's schedule wasn't opening up either. After a couple of weeks of trying to figure out our schedules, we finally found a day that worked for both of us.

Anyone with kids understands that no matter how much you plan, you always have the kid factor. It is the little cloud that hovers over every plan you make, and you never know whether something will happen with the kids that will change your plans. Well, the week we set aside to head to the cabin and finish things, the sick bug found Tim's family, and it wouldn't leave. The day we planned to leave, Tim's kids threw up all morning. Sigh. Do we go or do we stay?

With blessings from Tim's wife, we decided to go.

When we arrived at the cabin (after a short spell arguing with Google Maps over the cabin's actual location) and settled in, we started talking about you, the reader, and how we wanted you to interact with the book. We decided to write an opening that might serve as a short encouragement.

While you read this book, life will continue. Maybe your kids will throw up (although we hope not!), work will seem overwhelming, or school will keep you up all night. Through all of this, beauty exists.

Take a minute and pray that God will use your time with this book to show you the beauty all around you. Pray that he will give you conversations that bring out the beauty in your life and the lives of your family and friends. Pray the message of the book encourages specific people you know, and ask God to use you to communicate what you are learning to them.

And don't forget to pray for yourself!

DISCUSSION

Ask your group of friends to pray for you as you read the book. Tell them you are praying for them too.

Chapter 1: Discussion

We, the Brilliance Makers

REFLECTION

In chapter 1 we wanted you to sit next to Tim during his wintry car ride to meet friends for early morning breakfast. We wanted you to feel the different colors rising from the horizon—almost as if God were sketching with a No. 2 pencil and colored chalk. We wanted you to gasp with us about the quiet brilliance we encounter every morning—the beauty of life, the wonder of friendships, and the tension of where it all sits in a world that fractures the brilliance.

Read Psalm 84 (NIV). Pay attention to verse 11. The poet here describes God as the sun: "The LORD God is a sun and shield; / the LORD bestows favor and honor."

Reflect on God as the sun. Think about the characteristics of the sun. How it rises and chases the dark into the western horizon. How by it, we see the world. How it reveals. How it heals. How it warms. How it causes plants and trees to grow. How it creates beauty through light. How it spans the landscape and covers everything.

A prayer:

Lord, you shine into my life like the sun. You chase away the dark each morning. Great is your faithfulness! You are new and the same every morning, like the sun. Thank you for how you grow me through your Holy Spirit. Thank you for how you heal me through your Sweet Comforter. Thank you for how you reveal the shadows of my life to me with warmth and tenderness.

Strengthen me to shine as you shine. Help me to give you glory in all things even as I find your glory in everything.

In Jesus' name, amen.

DISCUSSION

How well do you think the Christian community at large, in this country, does with shining the brilliance in culture? Instead of pointing a finger at certain leaders or organizations, what can you and your small group or local church do to be a consistent beam of brilliance in your community?

In order to be brilliance makers, we must first pursue a real and deep relationship with Jesus. Our action stems from our affections. This may cause you to be more transparent than you're used to, but that's okay. You won't melt away by sharing your heart. Discuss your affections, or lack thereof, for Jesus. What stymies you in your walk with him: overwork, too much schoolwork and playtime, kids who keep you on your toes all day, the stress of running a house, the pressure of running a business, the impetus to make it in a world that constantly changes?

How does the element of trust factor into your taking the time to nurture your spiritual affections? Sometimes we push ourselves and stress ourselves because we fail to trust Jesus—we forget that he loves us more than the sparrow. How much do you trust him?

Before you delve into the rest of the chapters, it's good to establish a foundation of thought. Discuss how important it is to understand *who God is*—altogether true, altogether good, and altogether beautiful—and what his glory means to us in our everyday lives before we set out to conquer the world. Isn't it just enough to rest in the peace of his glory? (Not saying we should never *do* anything, but you get the point.)

Brutalized

REFLECTION

As we wrote this discussion guide, our church experienced the loss of a member in a car accident. The member served as a leader in the community and in the church, the type of guy who always had a kind word to share, a helping hand to lend, and a huge smile to give. He led a small group with the first graders and played in the youth band. He was only seventeen.

Why God? Why? Why would you allow this shadow to cast itself? What good is this? We want your will, but we want our children to be safe. Just do it that way.

The accident happened on a Saturday. The next morning our church overflowed with people. Our pastor led us through the gospel message of hope and resurrection. There, with the rest of us, sat the boy's parents. When asked how they could make it to church after something so tragic, they responded, "Where else would we be? This is our church family."

Would you go to church the day after the death of your son? Or would you crawl up in a ball and hide? Would you curse God? Be honest with yourself. How would you respond?

A parent burying his or her child, the darkest of shadows that life can cast. Yet it happens. What shadows have cast over your life? How did you respond? Did you find beauty in that moment? Why could you? Or why couldn't you?

Read 2 Corinthians 4:6–18. This passage is our brilliance maker theme passage. What does Paul say about our current struggles in this life? Why do we struggle to maintain this perspective?

DISCUSSION

Brace yourself: this discussion could take a while, and it might feel a tad uncomfortable. We tend to keep our hurts and pains and dark moments to ourselves. But we want you to open up and share. Use discernment, of course, but share a time of lost innocence with the group. Or maybe a time when you acted more like the culture and less like Christ. It's okay. We all have pain, and we have moments we aren't proud of.

Don't share only the shadow of your circumstance or past experience; share the beauty you saw in the midst of the pain. If you can't see it, that's okay. Share that too.

As a group, celebrate the beauty found, and thank God that the shadow faded (or will one day).

Take a moment to read and discuss Revelation 21:1–8. In this beautiful, yet haunting, passage John the Beloved shows us a glimpse of the coming hope of Christ himself. How does this passage encourage you? How can you use verse 4 as a source of hope for others who are struggling through the shadows?

In the chapter we quote scholar Peter Kreeft, who discusses our Christian hope. Kreeft said, "Hope means that our heads do not bump up against the low ceiling of this world; hope means that the exhilarating, wonderful, and terrifying winds of Heaven blow in our ears." Discuss what that means for you in your daily life.

As Christians, if we have hope in what is to come, how should that affect our outlook on our lives, society, and so forth? If we lived this hope, how would our engagement with culture differ from that of the rest of the world?

What would the world look like if we acted the way you just described? Identify times you can remember when Christians took a stand against culture in a winsome and attractive way.

Are there ways you can push back on society? Careful, we don't want to retreat from society; we want to work from within. Can you offer something different, unique, and brilliant in response? How? Be specific.

We talked about society and how it seems determined to steal our innocence. As adults, what are some ways you can fight this? Think about the media you consume or where you spend your time or money.

Does anyone in your group have kids? How can the community work together to help them keep their innocent eyes as long as possible?

Chapter 3: Discussion

Brilliance Unseen

REFLECTION

Jason's restaurant encounter happened about a year before this chapter was written. But it was one of those experiences that kept coming up. It took a year to unpack that encounter and all its layered meanings. The unpacking isn't over.

How often do we pass over a moment and hurry on to the next thing? Maybe we miss the beauty because we don't have the time to think and reflect and listen. Do you think that's true in your life?

Have you ever encountered something beautiful yet unexpected, like the girl in the restaurant? This week think about what you felt during your encounter and why it was so unexpected.

We were talking one day and lingered on this idea that the Holy Spirit lives inside us. We were all taught this on day one of being a Christian. But sometimes it can seem so abstract. As we talked about it, we couldn't get over the idea of how powerful the Holy Spirit is, and if he resides in us, we must have that too. (Jason kept repeating, "That's nuts!")

Think about it: *the* Holy Spirit resides inside you as a Christian. Can you comprehend the awesomeness of this truth? Do you see that you have the brilliance? How does this knowledge affect your prayer life? Your decision making? Your day-to-day faith? Reflect on all of this.

In chapter 1 we say that "to be a *brilliance maker* means to live differently." Remember the Holy Spirit living inside us? That makes us brilliance makers! What does that look like for you? What is different in your context?

What does brilliance do to darkness? It dispels it. It washes it away. It reveals the previously unseen. It exposes. If *the brilliance* can be used as another term for the gospel message of Jesus, evaluate how brilliant the gospel shines in your life: in your talk, in your work, in your relationships, in your play.

DISCUSSION

Talk about the most beautiful song or painting or poem or picture you can think of. Try to describe it as best you can. Then show it or listen to it or read it. Did everyone else see what you saw? Feel what you felt? Did others appreciate it the way you did?

As a group discuss the ideas of beauty. After your show-and-tell would you say beauty is objective or subjective? Or maybe a little of both? Support your claim. This discussion never resolves with us.

Ask group members to share where they see beauty in their different life and work contexts. (That is, where does your accountant friend see beauty and how does that compare to your teacher friend or your barista friend?) What rules do you have to obey in order to be good at your job? And how has your perspective of beauty changed as your life has changed? Has age or circumstance or kids changed what you see as beautiful?

Now that you have shared something beautiful, do you see any connections among the group? Maybe you all liked the same song or have a change in perspective due to similar life experiences? Or maybe you all have similar rules that govern your work? Once you see the connections, do you see obvious ways your group can be brilliance makers? What can you do together? And what about your church or small group?

Our actions should always be supported by thoughtful theology. So, what is the theology of a brilliance maker? Said another way, what does God say about the way his light shines in you and through you? After you gain some *understanding* of what that means, incorporate ideas. Don't get all fancy; start simple. How does being a brilliance maker affect our corporate worship gathering? Maybe you've been putting off involvement in a local cause or charity. Maybe you should stop stalling. Based on this discussion, we bet you have some things in common that could spark ideas.

A Rocket Ship to God *and* Mist Kiss

REFLECTION

When we pray, our posture looks like someone kneeling in submission. We bow our heads and extend our arms, palms face up. This signals a surrendering. Our physical posture mimics a spiritual expression: "Enough is enough—you're in control. I have nothing. My hands open for you. Take it all."

In these moments of worship and in our lives, we release what we have to God. We throw down our nets and follow him in recognition that all we have is his and he is all. Jason's wife often repeats the wisdom of what Corrie ten Boom said, "Hold everything in your hands lightly, otherwise it hurts when God pries your fingers open" (*Everyday Matters Bible for Women* [Peabody, MA: Hendrickson, 2012], 754).

In all of this our empty hands draw us closer to Christ. Like the empty bowl Hara uses as an example, we enter into a transitional state. We call it "sanctification."

In this metamorphosis we grow more and more like Christ. We take on his image, allowing the power of the Spirit to work within us as we continue to confess and surrender.

During the next week, look for the possibilities waiting in your life. Not wishful thinking but plans you think God has waiting for you. Are you conforming God to your will, like the ergonomic handle of the Western steak knife? Or do you resemble the empty possibility of the Japanese steak knife?

As you pray today and over the next several days—maybe the next month—ask God to remove your cynical eyes and replace them with those of a child. Ask him to help you believe again. Ask him to show you possibility. Ask him to help you release whatever you hold on to and open your hands.

We think you'll be surprised.

DISCUSSION

Contrast the story in chapter 2 of the childhood lingerie with Lyric's imaginary encounter with God.

What are you cynical about? Start with something silly. Maybe you are cynical about the buy-one-get-one advertisement the grocery store runs on Tuesdays because you know you don't need two boxes of frosted cereal and never would have bought them if it weren't for the coupon. Start with something like that advertisement.

Now move to something a bit deeper. What about your friend who never apologized for missing your party? Now dig more. What else? Keep digging. Are you cynical about your faith? Do you really think God hears you when you pray? Can you really see God?

With all that, small and big, do you think God can work in your life to help you regain some of your innocence? Or are you cynical about that too? Can you really see the world through the eyes of a child?

Can you think of a time when you felt God reach down and encourage you? When was it? What did it feel like? Were you cynical in that moment?

Now think of a time when you were emptied. What was it? How did that feel?

For Jason, it took a day of hiking and a daughter who believed in something. Do you need those grand moments with God to move past the cynics? If so, then discuss some ways your group can help each other find those moments. Jason saw a girl in a restaurant and also visited Yosemite. Both instances differ in scale and form and outcome, but both required a certain perspective that looked at the world in a different way.

Do you think you can return to a state of innocence, a blank slate, if you will, with God and with the world?

How can you practice looking at the world with innocence and renewed perspectives?

Chapter 6: Discussion

An Ostrich, a Mystery, and the Wail of Contentment

REFLECTION

In the Old Testament, we see the importance of the memorial stone.

After Moses died, Joshua was announced leader of the Israelites. In Joshua 3 God performs a miracle by blocking the water from the flooding Jordan, allowing the Israelites to cross. In Joshua 4 God instructs Joshua to choose twelve men, one from each tribe of Israel, to select a stone from the river and lay them down near the camp. Why? So that the generations to follow will remember how God provided.

Imagine one day pointing out to your children and grand-children all the ways God provided for you. Jason once said that if he built a memorial in his yard every time he wanted to remember God's work in his life, he wouldn't have to mow his yard anymore because of all the memorials. Then he'd need to build another memorial in thanks for not having to mow the lawn.

Reflect on your life and all that God has done. For what do you need to thank him? What are some big things God has done in your life? Write those things down, thinking of each line like a memorial stone.

Now that you have counted what the Lord has given, can you count what he has taken away? Go ahead and write them down too.

Is the "take away" list easier to compile or harder? It's okay either way, but we would love for you to think through the connections between the two lists. Maybe you lost a job (the Lord took), which led to a job that required less travel and more time with the family (the Lord gave).

While working on this book, both of us were in the process of selling our homes. A family relocating to the Atlanta area made an offer on Tim's house. Tim and his wife were ecstatic; the price was in line with what they needed in order to feel good about the sale, and selling the house confirmed that God wanted them to move (the Lord gave). Several days after the acceptance of the offer, Tim was driving to the grocery store when his real estate agent called. The other family backed out of the contract (the Lord took). Tim pulled into a parking spot and prayed: *Why, God, did you take this offer away? Why aren't you selling this house?*

Tim drove home and reported the news to his wife. She didn't understand either why God would do this. They spent the next hour praying and reading devotions together. They told God that he would have to do more than that to get them mad at him. They once again released the sale of the house into his hands. What else could they do but surrender?

In Tim's story Randall says that he had to lay his son down

and walk out of the room; it was a bold gesture in an extreme circumstance. Could you do that? What about something smaller in comparison, such as the sale of a house? Or a lost job?

What do you need to lay down in order to move toward thankfulness? Can laying it down bring you to contentment? Does control keep you from understanding God's work? Does it keep you from finding contentment?

DISCUSSION

Share some of the memorials you listed in your reflection time. Together, thank God for his provisions. Tell your friends why you are thankful for them. Celebrate one another. As friends, pray and thank God for one another. Repeat often!

Ask your friends, "What did God take from you that you can't get over?" It's a heavy question. Here's an equally heavy one to ask: "Have you ever cursed God?"

Remember how Jason's eyes were opened by the innocence of his daughter hiking through Yosemite? How do you think innocence helps you find contentment? What connection do you see between those ideas?

Spend time in prayer and thank God for his ultimate control and for all the ways he has provided for you. Read your list aloud to him as praise for his divine plan.

Chapters 7 and 8: Discussion

A Barbed Wire Horizon *and* The Weightlessness of Love

REFLECTION

Bad things happen to all of us. Some of us experience deep, deep pain and loss and hurt. Others of us, in comparison, lead blessed lives. The measure of the pain isn't the point. What matters is how those instances shape you. Do you crawl back into your cave and refuse to heal? Or do you step out and let God take over?

How do you think innocent eyes help you forgive? Can that new perspective help you shed the baggage you've dragged through life and see again, for the first time? Does cynicism bring you closer to or farther from forgiveness (of yourself and others)? Why?

As you reflect on these chapters we challenge you to think about times when you have wronged others. Have you reached out to your heavenly Father and asked forgiveness? Has someone wronged you? Have you reached out to your heavenly Father and asked for healing? Have you forgiven?

Our pastor, Jon Adams, preached a sermon on forgiveness that provides insights we thought we should pass on. Jon talked about Jesus gathering with his disciples in Capernaum. Jesus just finished rebuking his disciples for their competitive spirits. He called them to be humble like children and taught them the process of how to deal with a person who sins against you. Peter jumped in on the conversation: "Lord, how often will my brother sin against me, and I forgive him? As many as seven times?" (Matt. 18:21).

Jesus offered guidance on how to deal with someone who sins against you, but Peter persisted in asking how many times he should forgive. The rabbis' interpretation of the Old Testament was that someone was required to forgive three times, and after the fourth offense, he was no longer required to forgive. Peter thought, *I'm going to be more than generous with forgiveness and declare that I will forgive my brother seven times when he sins against me.* Jesus responded, "I do not say to you seven times, but seventy-seven times" (Matt. 18:22).

Forgiveness has no limit; it's inexhaustible, and you must forgive relentlessly. Jesus told the parable of the servant whose king forgave his debts (Matt. 18:23–35). In today's currency, the debt the servant owed was around $900 million. The king forgave, but the servant would not forgive someone who owed him the equivalent of $60 today.

We live in a bottomless hole of debt. When Jesus told this story about a big debt and a little debt, he taught about the big debt of sins (we have) versus the little debt (those who sin against us).

In the New Testament, there are five Greek words for *sin*. The words can mean missing the mark, trespass or slipping or falling, stepping across the line, or lawlessness. In this parable, Jesus uses the fifth Greek word for sin: *opheilema*, meaning "debt" (W. E. Vine, *Vine's*

Complete Expository Dictionary [Nashville: Thomas Nelson, 1996], 150, s.v. "debt"). Why is that important? When you sin against God, you can't pay the debt. You may not murder or cheat on your wife or rob a bank, but the separation between your sin and God and the separation between an adulterer and God are the same.

If you have been forgiven little, you give others even less forgiveness. If you can't forgive others, you think you deserve to hold on to anger or bitterness because you don't see yourself receiving much forgiveness.

In this parable Jesus says that the man tried to pay his debt by selling his wife and his children into slavery, but even by selling all he had, even his family, he could not pay this debt. Only Jesus' forgiveness, his work on the cross, covers the depth of our debt.

If you struggle with insecurity about God's forgiveness and love, you may feel that you're stuck in that hole of debt. And when you lack confidence in God's love and forgiveness, you will put your security in other things.

Think about when you fail to forgive someone else. It's usually something that has become overinflated in its importance to you. For example, it may be easy for you to forgive something like a little lie, but what if your spouse cheated on you or someone hurt your child? Would you destroy that person? Resent him or her forever? Could you forgive?

In the parable, the king forgave the debt because the servant pleaded with him. Then he asked, "Should not you have had mercy on your fellow servant, as I had mercy on you?"

Do you realize how deep your salvation runs? We owe far more than money to Christ, but we struggle to forgive others.

The psalmist wrote,

> Bless the LORD, O my soul,
>
> and all that is within me,
>
> bless his holy name!
>
> Bless the LORD, O my soul,
>
> and forget not all his benefits,
>
> who forgives all your iniquity,
>
> who heals all your diseases,
>
> who redeems your life from the pit. (Ps. 103:1–4)

The forgiving process begins with praise to our Lord and King, to our heavenly Father. Our praise resets our hearts and gives us the courage to look at the depth of our sin and to have the humility and faith to receive the depth of his salvation.

Remember these principles that come from Matthew 18. First, a lack of forgiveness imprisons us. We understand intuitively that anger and bitterness eat us alive emotionally and spiritually. The king handed the unforgiving servant over to the "jailers" (Matt. 18:34). The word here means "torturers." Our lack of forgiveness will imprison us and keep a distance between us and our offender and us and God.

Second, forgiveness is a willingness to absorb the cost of the debt. The whole point of this parable is that the king was willing to reach down and snatch the servant out of his huge debt. Are you willing to forgive others of their comparatively microscopic debts? This doesn't mean a willingness to allow destructive behaviors to continue; it means a willingness to ask the Holy Spirit to move our hearts toward compassion, to send away the offense of those who have offended.

Third, we need to center our forgiveness of others in Christ. Ephesians 4:32 describes it best: "Be kind and compassionate to one another, forgiving each other, just as in Christ God forgave you" (NIV). God forgave us Christians of everything.

DISCUSSION

When Jason's dad talks about his past, he talks about what God has done in his life. The past isn't a reminder of all the bad that happened; instead it serves as a marker for when God started doing all the hard work. What a beautiful idea, that the bad can turn to good and that all things can work to glorify God. Do you see the world that way? Talk as a group about times when bad circumstances turned to good. Thank God as a group for these redemptive slices of life.

Now, talk about the idea of forgiveness. Tim's dad said, "When the heart forgives, the mind no longer remembers." Is that possible? Another God-mystery? Or just a nice idea propagated by pastors?

Have any of your friends experienced a forgetting? Can you articulate what that felt like? How it worked?

As a group, pray the Lord's Prayer together. We like this version that Dallas Willard wrote in *The Divine Conspiracy* ([New York: HarperCollins, 2009], 269):

> Dear Father always near us,
>
> may your name be treasured and loved,
>
> may your rule be completed in us—

May your will be done here on earth

in just the way it is done in heaven.

Give us today the things we need today,

and forgive us our sins and impositions on you

as we are forgiving all who in any way offend us.

Please don't put us through trials,

but deliver us from everything bad.

Because you are the one in charge,

and you have all the power,

and the glory too is all yours—forever—

which is just the way we want it!

Chapter 9: Discussion

Life as Dance and the Brush Fire of Brilliance

REFLECTION

After Tim's beach encounter we headed to a local dive for chips and salsa. We talked about the idea of a dance wading out into the unknown and what that means. We discussed dancing versus stamping around and how you sometimes can't tell the difference.

Like Peter when he wanted to storm the gates, he probably felt that he was helping Jesus, but in reality he was just stamping around.

Do you feel that you are dancing with God or stamping your feet in resistance?

Chips and salsa couldn't resolve all the reasons we sometimes decide to keep our boots on and stay in the sand. We know that all of us have root sins, sins behind the sin, like control or approval.

When you decide to stamp instead of dance, what do you think is the reason? When you dance, why? Can you tell the difference?

DISCUSSION

If you live near a beach, you need to head there now, kick off your boots, and walk in the water. For the rest of you, recall the last time you were at the beach.

During your reflection time we asked you to think through core issues that incite you to stamp. Would you share your thoughts? Use the discussion to encourage one another and offer insights you have learned from your life.

Where do you see beauty springing up in your life? What does it look like for you? Maybe an early morning cup of coffee with just you and your thoughts or time spent with your family talking about "the old days"? Do you see it at a deeper level, maybe the healing you experienced from some pain in your past?

How can the people in the conversation encourage one another? Perhaps one among you sees beauty in places that others don't. If so, ask that person to serve as a beauty-spotting partner for you, looking for beauty in your life and showing it to you. We don't think you'll regret it.

For those of you at the beach, kick some water on your friend and then run to the car.

Chapter 10: Discussion

Living in Delight

REFLECTION

This past summer Jason turned over the mowing duties to his oldest son. Jason still trimmed and edged, but Ethan took the bulk of the yard, and he hated it. Some Saturdays it took hours just to work through the attitude and punishments to finally crank the mower. Jason did his best to make a game of it, allowing his son to mow over certain things like old toys and sidewalk chalk. That helped!

After one Saturday of mowing, Jason was standing on his front porch with his son, and a light summer rain fell. The fresh-cut grass sparkled in the raindrops. He looked at Ethan and said, "Son, look at that grass. Look at the straight lines and the perfect edge. Look how plush! We did that, buddy. Me and you, we worked, and we made the grass look like that. Isn't that cool? How cool that God allows us to work with him to make our little plot of land beautiful!"

As only an eleven-year-old boy can, Jason's son shrugged his shoulders and replied, "Whatever, I guess. Can I go play now?" Then he turned and walked inside.

How many times at your work have you thought, *Whatever,* turned in your report, and bolted home?

During that summertime lawn mowing, Jason bought *Every Good Endeavor* (New York: Dutton, 2012) by Timothy Keller. While reading the book, Jason shared excerpts during family devotions in hopes it would make the mowing more meaningful. Maybe it sank in and maybe it didn't, but for us as number crunchers and salespeople and mechanics and all the rest, consider this passage from Keller:

> If we are to be God's image-bearers with regard to creation, then we will carry on his pattern of work. . . . [His world] needs to be cultivated like a garden. . . . [W]e are to be *gardeners* who take an active stance toward their charge. They do not leave the land as it is. They rearrange it in order to make it most fruitful, to draw the potentialities for growth and development out of the soil. They dig up the ground and rearrange it with a goal in mind: to rearrange the raw material of the garden so it produces food, flowers, and beauty. And that is the pattern for all work. It is creative and assertive. . . .
>
> This pattern is found in all kinds of work. Farming takes the physical material of soil and seed and produces food. Music takes the physics of sound and rearranges it into something beautiful and thrilling that brings meaning to life. When we take fabric and make a piece of clothing, when we push a broom and clean a room, when we use technology to harness the forces of electricity, when we take an unformed, naïve human mind and teach it a subject, when we teach a couple how to resolve their relational disputes, when we take simple

materials and turn them into a poignant work of art—we are continuing God's work of forming, filling, and subduing. Whenever we bring order out of chaos, whenever we draw out creative potential, whenever we elaborate and "unfold" creation beyond where it was when we found it, we are following God's pattern of creative cultural development. (58–59, emphasis in original)

Thinking about work in this way may not make mowing the grass any easier, but it certainly gives it meaning. Tim mentioned that he felt alive when working on his Rover. What makes you feel alive? Is it your vocation? Your hobby? Both?

Speaking of hobbies, how do you spend your leisure time? How do you rest and exercise your mind?

This week monitor your time. What do you spend it on? And how are you working at worship during those times?

Now consider your vocation. How do you, or can you, glorify God in what you do? Does this translate to your free time as well? How? How not?

DISCUSSION

Our American context views work success in dollars and cents, maximizing our income as we step up the corporate ladder. The more we make, the more successful we become. This mind-set leads us toward a particular job or profession where success can be measured according to the metrics stipulated by a society.

Instead of asking, "How much money can I make?" what if we

asked, "How much can I contribute to the kingdom of God?" and "What am I uniquely wired to do?"

If you asked those questions, do you think you might receive a different answer? Discuss these ideas with your friends. Do you agree with our assessment? Disagree?

In the chapter, Tim suggests Sabbath rest does not come from inactivity; instead it comes from doing something. To Jason, changing the suspension on his car doesn't sound like Sabbath at all. It sounds more like the seventh ring of hell. But mowing the yard, working on that never-ending side project, picking blueberries, or grilling out with friends sounds more like Sabbath to Jason. What do you think about that view of Sabbath? How do you rest?

Tell your friends how you glorify God in your work and in your rest. Celebrate each other's work by expressing what you appreciate about it.

Chapter 11: Discussion

On Imagination

REFLECTION

Tim and I noticed we kept mentioning "imagination" in our discussions around the idea of beauty and brilliance. It occurred to us as we discussed chapter 10, "Living in Delight," that we should mention something about the importance of imagination, how story shapes its context and how our imaginations shape us.

Our imaginations represent a powerful tool. How we steward them matters. What we allow in them matters. What comes out of them matters.

Take a moment to meditate on Proverbs 4:23: "Guard your heart, for it is the wellspring of life" (NIV).

What does your heart look like? And when we say heart, we mean the all of you that we spoke about in the chapter. Is your heart dark? Is it light? Do you feel far from God? Close? Why do you feel this way?

Have you been a good steward of your imagination? Or have you allowed the world to move it away from brilliance?

What stories shape you the most? Stories from television, film, or contemporary fiction? Is it explicitly wrong to indulge in these mediums? How do we guard against the invading shadows stemming from the dim stories of the world?

DISCUSSION

Discuss your media viewing habits. If you have a family, what does your television regimen or diet look like? What evidence do you see in yourself that might tell you your imagination has been hijacked? If you have children, do you talk about the stories and programs they watch via film and television? How do you offset the shadow-filled stories that inundate their lives?

How do you think you may find balance in media intake and spiritual intake? Are there physical consequences to letting your imagination be overrun by different forms of media? What other types of media make it difficult to revitalize your imagination?

To Kill a Mockingmouse or Something for Wives to Pass to Their Husbands

REFLECTION

Think about your dad. Did he model manliness for you? Good and bad, what can you learn from him?

What do you think defines a *godly man*?

Would you consider yourself selfish? What about the little things, like grabbing the last cookie from the jar? Do you ever feel that you miss out on things because of your attitude? Have you ever ignored God because it seemed too much work to follow him?

The Bible offers Proverbs 31 for women but nothing that specific for men. Why do you think that is? What biblical examples of manliness can you think of?

Pray for the men and boys in your life. Thank God for them, and ask him to continue molding and shaping them.

Men, think through younger men in your life. What are ways you can start to disciple other guys (kids, coworkers, neighbors)?

Women, think about how you can validate the idea of a real man.

DISCUSSION

Women, what do you think about this chapter? Men, do your best to pipe down during this part. You will have your chance in a minute.

Men, tell the group about a man who invested in your life, someone like your dad or a pastor or a good friend. What made him stand out to you? Why was that relationship important? How did it affect the way you view yourself as a man?

Men, based on your experiences and relationships, do you agree with this chapter? Why or why not?

We offer a perspective of what a man looks like by riffing from Proverbs 31. As a group, read Proverbs 31:10–31 aloud. Stop after each verse and discuss it. Then read our Proverbs 32 and stop after each stanza and discuss it. Do you see parallels? What are they? Do you agree with us? Disagree?

Agree with us or not, talk about what a real, godly man looks like. What can your group do to show that version of manliness to society? Use your imaginations (hey, you just read about that!) to describe a world where men act like men. What would be different? What would be better?

As Christians, we have hope for that kind of place. It's beautiful, yeah?

Chapter 13: Discussion

The Sound and the Fury

REFLECTION

Tim's reflection here on the need for family and friends touches emotions we all feel at some point. We love our families, but the miles separate us. We're devoted to our friends, but time moves us from college fun to newlywed craziness to the land of crazy children and work pressures. And yet their love is the one thing we continually long for.

This piece is short enough to read twice. So we suggest you do so. Read it through with your coffee or beverage of choice. Then read it again out loud—but not in a public place or else people will think you're an oddball. Tim may do this, but you shouldn't!

After you read it out loud, reflect on your relationships with your family—your immediate family first, then your extended family. Is there something between you and your siblings, your parents, or your spouse? Is it something that rests on you to initiate so that it can be resolved? What keeps you from resolving it?

Maybe you can't relate to loving your family with any depth

because you've been hurt so deeply. Ask God for the strength to endure and the strength to move on from the hurt and into the land of reconciliation and healing. Sometimes we carry things around when we really just need to lay them at the foot of the cross. Is there something you need to lay down right now?

DISCUSSION

Share a time of relational winter with your group. Maybe you're in it now and haven't shared it with anyone. Now would be a good time to share the very thing keeping you from reaching out to those you love.

Use your group time to share specific pain, pain that can find comfort from a group member who's endured a similar situation. In order to know this, however, you must all share with guarded transparency. Remember, share time isn't gossip time or time to hold the conch for the duration of the group. Transparency means to let others see into your need. This is how we help one another: we share without pretense, and we aid without judgment.

Remind yourselves what love means. For your next group time, type the verses to 1 Corinthians 13. Now, on the back of the paper, write out the chapter in your own words. Here's a sample of what it may read like:

If I have special talents that nobody else has, but I don't possess love, then when I act in my talents I am just a big gong—making noise with no point.

Chapter 14: Discussion

Oak Shadows and Autumn Sun

REFLECTION

Memorize the Frost poem "Stopping by Woods on a Snowy Evening." Just kidding. But if you read it, you won't be sorry.

When you think back over your life, what images lie engraved in your memory? Are some of the shadows in those memories? Can you measure your good memories against the bad ones? Do you find more good or bad memories? How do you think this affects how you see things in the present?

This chapter marks the end of the book. What are three major things God has shown you while reading this book? They can be unrelated to the book, but think through the last couple of weeks. What are they?

How has the dynamic with your friends or group changed over the past couple of weeks? Name a person or two whom you have grown to appreciate more as a result of your discussions.

By the way, we talked about sanctification earlier in this guide.

In case you ever have doubts about your walk with Christ, this is what sanctification looks like.

DISCUSSION

Share your earliest memory with the group. Retell the memory as you would a scene in a book. Describe it in vivid detail, doing your best to make the others feel the way you felt. Were there any common experiences or feelings? How does returning to that place in your mind make you see things differently today?

In the discussion for chapter 2 we asked you to share some of the shadows in your life. We hope that you were able to point to the beauty you found as well. Celebrate all the good things in your life. Just the good. The day you met your spouse, the day your kids were born, the time you found a twenty-dollar bill in your pants pocket, the healing you experienced, or maybe the answer to a prayer.

As a group, can you start to point out the good you see to one another? In your reflection time you listed ways you have grown to appreciate one another. Share that with the group. Encourage one another.

Spend some time in prayer.

Father,

The world is broken and dark, but you are complete light. Through you we see past the hurt and pain and daily defeats and we see the eternal beam of beauty. We ask that you pull us from the shadows. Heal our pains. Lighten our loads. Give us rest.

In our lives, our community, our families, as it is in heaven.

Amen.

Acknowledgments

To those who shape our thoughts—thank you: The Son of God, Jon Adams, Christine Willard, Heather Locy, Dr. Alister McGrath, Eddie Vedder, The Inklings, Dale, Colorado Mountains, Brooklyn sidewalks, and Oxford pastures.

To the early adopters—Christopher Ferebee for your guidance, honesty, and most of all your friendship throughout this process. Gabe Lyons for pushing us toward expressing our thoughts and ideas and validating our efforts.

To those who took the time to read through rough ideas or offer feedback and comments—thank you: Adam Webber, Seth and Amber Haines, Brian and Mandy Miller, Jean Crane, Dave Blanchard, Kary Oberbrunner, Brent Cole.

To those who continue to support, encourage, and lend a helping hand along the way—thank you: Brad Lomenick, Ken Coleman, Scott Calgaro, Kenny Jahng, Jonathan Merritt, Lacey and Joshua Sturm, Scott Kauffmann, Steve Graves, Ryan O'Neal, Jason Haynes, Joy Eggerichs, Esther Fleece, Lauren Taylor Baker, Trinity Laurel, Cortney Aranda, Jessica Hoffman, Paul Phipps Victor, and Dixie Oliver.

To the team at Thomas Nelson who saw something worth printing—thank you: Angela Scheff, Janene MacIvor, Julie Faires, Kimberly

Boyer, Joel Miller, and all the rest of the team behind the scenes working on our behalf. We owe you all a coffee (or whatever it is they drink at Thomas Nelson).

***

I (Tim) would like to extend a special thanks to Jason Locy, for the grace to be a silly poet, for unwavering friendship, and for taking punches until their will grows tired. Here's to writing the story of life—don't forget to track your changes. To Marlene and Ken Mottin, my "in-laws," my friends. This book would not exist if not for the all the times you climbed in "ye old Rover" and took the kids out for "Mogli-Mogli." Forever in your debt! To my family, their spouses and children—it's hard being a brother, a son, and an uncle from England. Thank you for encouraging me with your prayers. To John Adams for listening to me rant while Jason horked down waffles. To Brian and Mandy Miller for the flower of friendship and the push to dream. To Brent, you know why. To Steve Graves for your "energy" and your at-dusk-fly-fishing-conversation. To Gabe, for remaining, always. To Holly and Jessie for fire of Oban talks that minister so deeply to me. To my little pixies: to Lyric for making sure I "write it down," to Brielle for always wanting to sing, to Zion for the way you fill a room when you laugh. For my wife, Christine: for walking in the Land of Brilliance with me, I experience more because you help me to *see*. I love you.

I (Jason) would like to extend a special thanks to Tim Willard, a forever-grace-giver for those who do not track changes and for being a pretty good "mate, yeah." You carried a heavy load on this one, thank you. Gabe Lyons for thirty years of friendship and support. You are a brother. Patricio Juarez, Teresa Carter, and the rest of the FiveStone gang for picking up the slack while I worked on the book. Jon Adams, for taking the time to eat waffles with a punk. The Dieffenbachers, thank you for always lending a helping hand. Even when it means sitting in traffic on Flatbush. To Mom and Dad for allowing me to share our story. God claims it all for His glory, you prove it. My brother Josh for honest dialogue and accepting my supreme Lordship over Catan. Ethan, thanks for letting me walk you to school. Christian, thanks for reminding me to laugh. Naomi, thank you for dance parties. Eliana, they say the early bird gets the worm, thanks for making sure I always get the worm. Heather, I love you more than the ants love our kitchen. Thank you for always pointing me to God's brilliance. I love you.

Notes

Quotation

   C. S. Lewis, *Till We Have Faces* (San Diego: Harcourt Brace, 1984), 75; the speaker is Psyche.

CHAPTER 1: WE, THE BRILLIANCE MAKERS

Epigraphs:

   David the psalmist, Psalms 36:9.
   Fyodor Dostoyevsky, *The Idiot*, trans. Constance Garnett (New York: Macmillan, 1915), 556.
   Saint Augustine, *The Confessions* (Oxford, UK: Oxford University Press, 2008), 276.

 1. This is a reference to T. S. Eliot's poem "The Hollow Men" cited in Harold Bloom, ed., *T. S. Eliot* (Philadelphia: Chelsea House, 2003), 108. Eliot ends the poem with these lines: "This is the way the world ends / Not with a bang but a whimper." The reference to Psyche's sister comes from C. S. Lewis's masterpiece *Till We Have Faces*. The beautiful Psyche (Lewis's protagonist) has a sister who is ugly. She loves Psyche but struggles with intense jealousy.
 2. Definitions for Medieval Christian Liturgy: *Sanctus*, http://www.yale.edu/adhoc/research_resources/liturgy/d_sanctus.html.
 3. Ibid.
 4. C. S. Lewis, "Is Theology Poetry?" in *The Weight of Glory* (New York: HarperCollins, 1980), 140.
 5. Psalm 36:9 (KJV).
 6. 2 Corinthians 3:18 (MSG).
 7. Revelation 1:17.
 8. For more on the perplexing concept of beauty, see Lewis, *The Weight of Glory;* Cal Seerveld, *Rainbows for a Fallen World;* and Hans Urs von Balthasar, *The Glory of the Lord.* Philosopher Peter Kreeft says, "Beauty is known by the imagination; goodness, by conscience; and truth, by reason." *Back to Virtue* (San Francisco: Ignatius Press, 1992), 50.
 9. Acts 17:28 (NIV).
10. David F. Wright, Sinclair Ferguson, and J. I. Packer, eds., *New Dictionary of Theology* (Downers Grove, IL: InterVarsity Press, 1988), 38, s.v. "apologists."
11. J. I. Packer, *Knowing God* (Downers Grove, IL: InterVarsity Press, 1973), 127.

12. Saint Augustine, *Confessions* (Oxford, UK: Oxford University Press, 2008), 61.
13. "We all . . . are changed into the same image from glory to glory" (2 Cor. 3:18 KJV).
14. C. S. Lewis refers to beauty as a finger pointing to God. This theme emerges in several of his works, both fiction and nonfiction. Some writings you may want to access include: "Reflections in a Toolshed" (easily accessible in PDF format online); *Perelandra* and *Till We Have Faces* offer some of C. S. Lewis's most dynamic expressions of beauty within his fiction. "The Weight of Glory" address, which is found in *The Weight of Glory and Other Addresses*, is perhaps Lewis's most soaring exposition on beauty.
15. Saint Augustine, *Confessions*, 273.
16. This idea is communicated beautifully in John Mark McMillan's song "How He Loves." The line is: "When all of a sudden, I am unaware of these afflictions eclipsed by glory."

CHAPTER 2: BRUTALIZED

Epigraphs:

Emerson cited in Frank Crowell, *Man–God's Masterpiece* (New York: R. F. Fenno, 1916), 189.
W. B. Yeats, "The Stolen Child," in *Collected Poems of W. B. Yeats* (New York: Scribner, 1996), 18.
Thomas Merton, *Thoughts in Solitude* (New York: Farrar, Straus and Giroux, 1999), 38.

1. *UB Reporter*, University at Buffalo, The State University of New York, "Study Finds Marked Rise in Intensely Sexualized Images of Women" by Patricia Donovan, http://www.buffalo.edu/ubreporter/archive/2011_08_11/rolling_stone_images.html.
2. Hannah Arendt, *The Human Condition* (Chicago: University of Chicago Press, 1998), 134.
3. Andreas Kostenberger, ed., *Whatever Happened to Truth?* (Wheaton, IL: Crossway Books, 2005), 63. Timothy Keller discussed this at the Gospel Coalition's 2013 National Conference and writes about what he believes are the main elements of church revival in his book *Center Church: Doing Balanced, Gospel-Centered Ministry in Your City* (Grand Rapids: Zondervan, 2012).
4. J. I. Packer, *Knowing God* (Downers Grove, IL: InterVarsity Press, 1973), 128.
5. Friedrich Nietzsche, *The Selected Writings of Friedrich Nietzsche* (Radford, VA: Wilder Publications, 2008), 568.
6. John 3:19–21 (MSG).
7. Kostenberger, *Whatever Happened to Truth?*, 131.
8. Hebrews 1:3 (NIV).
9. Peter Kreeft, *Back to Virtue* (San Francisco: Ignatius Press, 1992), 74.
10. Frederick Buechner, *The Hungering Dark* (New York: HarperCollins, 1985), 123.
11. Proverbs 11:12.

12. Tim Challies, "In Which I ask Ann Voskamp's Forgiveness," Challies.com, May 28, 2012, emphasis added, http://www.challies.com/articles/in-which -i-ask-ann-voskamkps-forgiveness.

13. Luke 6:45 (NLT).

14. Dallas Willard, *The Divine Conspiracy* (New York: HarperCollins, 1997), 144.

15. See Soren Kierkegaard, *Eighteen Upbuilding Discourses*.

16. Henri J. M. Nouwen, *In The Name of Jesus* (New York: Crossroad, 1989), 25.

17. William Wordsworth cited in Francis T. Palgrave, *The Golden Treasury* (New York: Macmillan, 1922), 291.

18. C. S. Lewis, *Till We Have Faces* (San Diego: Harcourt Brace, 1984), 22.

19. William Wordsworth cited in John Bartlett, *Bartlett's Familiar Quotations*, 16th ed. (Boston: Little Brown, 1992), 373; the quotation is from Wordsworth's preface to *Lyrical Ballads,* 2nd ed. (1800).

20. C. S. Lewis, "The Seeing Eye," in *Christian Reflections* (Grand Rapids, MI: Eerdmans, 1995), 168–69.

21. 1 Peter 2:16–17.

22. Ryan's definition of beauty came through an interview we conducted with Ryan on the subject. Used by permission of Ryan O'Neal.

CHAPTER 3: BRILLIANCE UNSEEN

Epigraphs:

Pablo Picasso cited in Robert I. Fitzhenry, ed., *The Harper Book of Quotations*, rev. ed. (New York: HarperCollins, 1993), 49.

Leonard Cohen, from the song "Anthem," http://www.leonardcohenfiles .com/album10.html.

G. K. Chesterton, *Chesterton Day by Day*, ed. Michael Perry (Seattle: Inkling Books, 2002), 17.

1. Read more: Josh Tyrangiel, "Keeping Up the Ghost," *Time*, November 21, 2004, http://www.time.com/time/magazine/article/0,9171,785365,000.html.

2. See Bob Boilen, "About a Song: 'Hallelujah'," All Songs Considered, NPR Music, August 19, 2008, http://www.npr.org/blogs/allsongs/2008/08 /about_a_song_hallelujah_1.html.

3. For more on the invisibleness of the beautiful see John Milbank's dazzling essay "Beauty and the Soul." He says, "We hold onto particular phrases in music; they haunt our memory, not because of their structure, but because of their ineffable 'soul,' which is only possible through structure, and yet 'takes off' from structure. We know that it takes off, because we can analogously convey the same or a kindred style in different and heterogenous structures." John Milbank, Graham Ward, and Edith Wyschogrod, ed., *Theological Perspectives on God and Beauty* (Harrisburg, PA: Trinity International Press, 2003), 27.

4. See Exodus 33–34.

5. Timothy Keller, *King's Cross: The Story of the World in the Life of Jesus* (New York: Dutton, 2011), 114.

6. 2 Corinthians 4:4 (MSG).

7. 2 Corinthians 4:5–6 (MSG).

8. *Merriam-Webster's Collegiate Dictionary*, 11th ed., s.v. "sic transit gloria mundi" in the section "Foreign Words and Phrases."

CHAPTER 4: A ROCKET SHIP TO GOD

Epigraphs:

Dallas Willard, *Hearing God* (Downers Grove, IL: InterVarsity Press, 2012), 283.

Ann Voskamp, "Starting Now? The End to the Cynicism," A Holy Experience, October 5, 2012, http//www.aholyexperience.com/2012/10 /starting-now-the-end-to-the-cynicism/.

Ralph Waldo Emerson cited in Randy Alcorn, *Eternal Perspectives* (Carol Stream, IL: Tyndale House, 2012), 15.

1. Abraham Joshua Heschel, *Moral Grandeur and Spiritual Audacity* (New York: Farrar, Straus and Giroux, 1997), 59.

2. G. K. Chesterton, *Orthodoxy* (Rockville, MD: Serenity Publishers, 2009), 62.

3. C. S. Lewis, *The Screwtape Letters* (New York: HarperCollins, 1996), 65. Chapter 13 in Lewis's classic is worth reflection. We forget the importance of taking a walk or reading a good book, and we forget that God wants us to enjoy these things. Too often the simple and most beautiful things are run over by the world and its greedy desire.

4. William Blake, "The Lamb," in *The Essential Blake*, introduction by Stanley Kunitz (New York: HarperCollins, 1987), 4.

5. Blake, introduction to "Songs of Experience," in *The Essential Blake*, 20.

6. John 3:3 (NLT).

7. John 16:21–22 (MSG).

8. Hebrews 11:1–2 (MSG).

9. I'm (Tim) reminded of C. S. Lewis's description of reading George MacDonald's book *Phantastes* for the first time. He said that it was like his imagination was baptized and that a kind of magic light fell on the landscape all around him. He began to see the world as it was intended, with a bit of holy light settling all around him. See C. S Lewis, *Surprised by Joy: The Shape of My Early Life* (New York; London: Harcourt Brace, 1995), 179.

10. Ezekiel 37:1–14.

11. Colossians 3:1–2 (MSG).

12. Soren Kierkegaard, *Fear and Trembling* (London: Penguin Books, 1985), 55. Don't be put off by Kierkegaard. This little book, for example, is a great devotional read and has soaring prose around faith.

13. Alister McGrath and Joanna Collicutt McGrath, *The Dawkins Delusion* (Downers Grove, IL: IVP Books, 2007), 19.

CHAPTER 5: MIST KISS

Epigraphs:

Ludlow was speaking of Yosemite in the 1800s. His words are cited in *American Paradise*, ed. John K. Howart (New York: Metropolitan Museum of Art, 1987), 388.

Cited in Matthew Sleeth, *Hope for Creation* (Grand Rapids, MI: Zondervan, 2010), 47.

John Muir, *Our National Parks* (Boston: Houghton Mifflin, 1901), 1. He was a Yosemite advocate and the founder of the Sierra Club.

1. Bunnell cited in Jeffrey P. Schaffer, *Yosemite National Park* (Berkeley, CA: Wilderness Press, 2006), 9.
2. Muir, *Our National Parks*, 56.
3. Henry David Thoreau, *Walden and Other Writings* (New York: Bantam, 2004), 182.
4. Henry David Thoreau, *The Journal of Henry D. Thoreau*, vol. 2 (New York: Dover, 1962), 488.
5. The example of the knife is one that Hara often uses. This particular quotation came from the talk "Emptiness" at ad agency Wieden+Kennedy in Portland, May 4, 2011. You can view the full talk here: http://vimeo.com/23418377. Two books by Kenya Hara, *White* and *Designing Design* (Zürich, Switzerland: Lars Müller Publishers, 2007), expand on the philosophy of emptiness.
6. Hara, *White* (Zürich, Switzerland: Lars Müller Publishers, 2009), 35.

CHAPTER 6: AN OSTRICH, A MYSTERY, AND THE WAIL OF CONTENTMENT

Epigraphs:

John Bunyan, *The Riches of Bunyan* (New York: American Tract Society, 1850), 239.

Dietrich Bonhoeffer, *Letters and Papers from Prison* (Minneapolis: Fortress Press, 2010), 238.

Brent Curtis and John Eldredge, *The Sacred Romance* (Nashville: Thomas Nelson, 2001), 200.

1. C. S. Lewis, "Meditations in a Toolshed," in *God in the Dock* (Grand Rapids, MI: Eerdmans, 1970), 213.
2. Jeremiah 29:4–11.
3. Jeremiah 29:5–7 (NIV).
4. D. A. Carson et al., eds., *New Bible Commentary: 21st Century Edition* (Downers Grove, IL: InterVarsity Press, 1994), 693.
5. Here the authors paraphrase the famous interaction between Jesus and Peter recorded in John 21:22–23. *The Message* puts it like this: "Jesus said, 'If I want him to live until I come again, what's that to you? You—follow me.'"
6. Job 39:13–18.
7. Job 39:18 (NIV).
8. In Job God talks about the leviathan and behemoth. There are many ideas as to what these creatures really are. More recent commentaries suggest that folks in the ancient Near East would have understood these creatures to be the crocodile (leviathan) and the hippopotamus (behemoth). But looking over the scope of the Bible, it is probably a supernatural creature, and in Job, God is making the point that some things that he created have no

usefulness to humans. And that is the point we're making here. Like the ostrich, which in many respects is a ridiculous, useless bird, the leviathan and behemoth—which happen to symbolize chaos and ferocity—are useless to us. Even so, God controls both. So, God is the God of the beautiful and the ridiculous and the chaotic and fierce. All give us a glimpse into God's character and that he cares for us. He is the God of it all, and yet through it all, he holds us. We are precious to him. Source: John H. Walton, Victor H. Matthews, and Mark W. Chavalas, *The IVP Bible Background Commentary: Old Testament*, Accordance electronic ed. (Downers Grove: InterVarsity Press, 2000), n.p.

9. Job 1:21.
10. Job 7:11 (NIV).
11. Job 42:5–6 (NIV), emphasis added.

CHAPTER 7: A BARBED WIRE HORIZON

Epigraphs:

Flannery O'Connor, "Wise Blood," in *Three* (New York: Signet, 1983), 85.

Henry Wadsworth Longfellow, "The Rainy Day," in *A Henry Wadsworth Longfellow Companion*, ed. Robert L. Gale (Westport, CT: Greenwood Press, 2003), 206.

William Faulkner, *As I Lay Dying* (New York: Vintage, 1990), 176; the character Addie is speaking.

1. Proverbs 5:1, 3–4, 8–9, 11–13 (NIV).
2. If you are looking for some great quiet-time reading or daily reflective reading, check out Kierkegaard's *Works of Love* or *Christian Discourses*. Kierkegaard often gets a bad rep for being too dense, but his devotional writings are beautiful and would be a great addition to your spiritual readings. Søren Kierkegaard et al., *Works of love* (New York: HarperPerennial, 2009). *Christian Discourses: The Crisis and a Crisis in the Life of an Actress* (Princeton Univ Pr, 2009).
3. For an excellent essay on forgiveness read C. S. Lewis, "On Forgiveness," in *The Weight of Glory* (New York: HarperCollins, 1980), 177–83. Lewis unpacks this idea there.
4. Matthew 18:21–35.

CHAPTER 8: THE WEIGHTLESSNESS OF LOVE

Epigraphs:

Martin Luther King Jr., *The Papers of Martin Luther King, Jr.*, vol. 6, *Advocate of the Social Gospel, September 1948–March 1963* (Berkeley: University of California Press, 2007), 488.

The apostle Peter, 1 Peter 4:8 (NIV).

1. Jeremiah 31:34 (NIV).
2. Søren Kierkegaard et al., *Works of Love* (New York: HarperPerennial, 2009), 169.

CHAPTER 9: LIFE AS DANCE AND THE BRUSH FIRE OF BRILLIANCE

Epigraphs:

King David, 2 Samuel 6:21–22 (NIV).

Henri J. M Nouwen, *Can You Drink the Cup?* (Notre Dame, IN: Ave Maria Press, 2006), 29. A great read for more communion with God.

William Wordsworth, *Poetical Works [of] Wordsworth; with Introductions and Notes,* New ed, Oxford Paperbacks, 192 (London: Oxford U.P., 1969), 460.

1. C. S. Lewis, *Till We Have Faces* (San Diego: Harcourt Brace, 1984), 75.

CHAPTER 10: LIVING IN DELIGHT

Epigraphs:

Thomas Edison cited in Orison Swett Marden, ed., *Little Visits with Great Americans,* vol. 1 (New York: Success Company, 1905), 28.

David Thomas cited in Abram Coleman, ed., *Proverbial Wisdom,* 3rd ed. (New York: Peter Eckler, 1903), 187.

John Calvin cited in Philip C. Almond, *Adam and Eve in Seventeenth-Century Thought* (Cambridge, UK: Cambridge University, 1999), 99.

1. Miroslav Volf, *A Public Faith: How Followers of Christ Should Serve the Common Good* (Grand Rapids, MI: Brazos Press, 2011), 55–74.
2. Ibid., 59.
3. Ibid., 62.
4. Ibid., 61.
5. Henry David Thoreau, *Walden with Thoreau's Essay "On the Duty of Civil Disobedience"* (Rockville, MD: Arc Manor, 2007), 9.
6. Alister McGrath, *The Intellectual World of C. S. Lewis* (London: Wiley-Blackwell, 2013), 139.
7. Hebrews 4:3.
8. Dr. Hugenberger was my professor of Theology of the Pentateuch at Gordon-Conwell Theological Seminary. This quote comes from a sermon he did on the Sabbath. The sermon was accessed from the church's archive.
9. Matthew Crawford, *Shop Class as Soulcraft* (New York: Penguin, 2009), 65–66.
10. This is the common definition for human flourishing as taken from Aristotle's fourth-century lectures, which later came to be known as *Nicomachean Ethics.* Check out this great little article on human flourishing. It brings Aristotle and Plato's thought into clarity and allows us to take Aristotle's thought and apply it in our lives. Electronic Source: http://noetic.org/blog/time-human-flourishing/.
11. David F. Wright, Sinclair Ferguson, and J. I. Packer, eds., *New Dictionary of Theology* (Downers Grove, IL: InterVarsity Press, 1988), 729, s.v., "work."
12. Proverbs 8:30–31 (NIV).

CHAPTER 11: ON IMAGINATION

Epigraphs:

Albert Einstein cited in Sarvananda Bluestone, *World Dream Book* (Rochester, VT: Destiny Books), 4.

"Interview with Philip Pullman," Scholastic Book Clubs, http://clubs-kids
.scholastic.co.uk/clubs_content/7922.

Stephen King, *Hearts in Atlantis* (New York: Pocket Books, 1999), 25, emphasis in original; the speaker is Tom.

1. Michael Reeves, *Delighting in the Trinity: An Introduction to the Christian Faith*
   (Downers Grove, IL: IVP Academic, 2012), 85.
2. W. E. Vine, *Vine's Complete Expository Dictionary* (Nashville: Thomas Nelson,
   1996), 108, s.v. "heart."
3. Proverbs 4:23 (NIV).
4. I. Howard Marshall, A. R. Millard, J. I. Packer, and D. J. Wiseman, *New
   Bible Dictionary* (Downers Grove, IL: IVP, 1996), 456, s.v. "heart." The Bible
   reference is Mark 12:30 (NIV). C. S. Lewis also refers to the use of heart" in
   such a fashion: "The Hebrew word which St. Paul represents by [*kardia*]
   would be more nearly translated 'Mind'; and in Latin, one who is *cordatus*
   is not a man of feeling but a man of sense," C. S. Lewis, *The Discarded Image*
   (Cambridge, UK: Cambridge University Press, 1994), 160.
5. The apostle Paul says we become children of the light, transferred from the
   kingdom of darkness (1 Thess. 5:5). It seems Paul was a distant relative of
   J. R. R. Tolkien.
6. Electronic Source: http://www.oxforddictionaries.com/definition/english
   /imagination?q=imagination.
7. Gregory Bassham, "Lewis and Tolkien on the Power of the Imagination,"
   in David Baggett, Gary R. Habermas, and Jerry L. Walls, eds., *C. S. Lewis
   as Philosopher: Truth, Goodness and Beauty* (Downers Grove, IL: IVP Academic,
   2008), 245–47. Bassham here uses Immanuel Kant's divisions of the imagination traditionally referred to as the *reproductive* and *productive* types.
8. Kevin J. Vanhoozer, *First Theology* (Downers Grove, IL: IVP Academic,
   2002), 36.
9. Timothy Williamson, "Reclaiming the Imagination," *New York Times*, August
   15, 2010, http://opinionator.blogs.nytimes.com/2010/08/15/reclaiming
   -the-imagination/.
10. Matthew 13:34.
11. Bassham, "Lewis and Tolkien on the Power of the Imagination," 250–52.
12. The Barna Group has produced stunning data regarding the moral direc-
    tion of our country: "'We are witnessing the development and acceptance
    of a new moral code in America,' said the researcher and author, who
    has been surveying national trends in faith and morality for more than
    a quarter-century. 'Mosaics have had little exposure to traditional moral
    teaching and limited accountability for such behavior. The moral code
    began to disintegrate when the generation before them—the Baby
    Busters—pushed the limits that had been challenged by their parents—the
    Baby Boomers. The result is that without much fanfare or visible leader-
    ship, the U.S. has created a moral system based on convenience, feelings,
    and selfishness.'" The reference in the text and this quotation come from
    "a New Moral Code," Barna Group, August 25, 2008, https://www.
    barna.org/teens-next-gen-articles/25-young-adults-and-liberals-struggle
    -with-morality/.

13. J. R. R. Tolkien, "On Fairy-Stories," in *Poems and Stories* (New York: Houghton Mifflin, 1994), 170–71.
14. Alister McGrath, *The Intellectual World of C. S. Lewis* (London: Wiley-Blackwell, 2013), 73.
15. Peter Kreeft, "Lewis's Philosophy of Truth, Goodness, and Beauty," in *C. S. Lewis as Philosopher: Truth, Goodness and Beauty*, ed. Baggett, Habermas, and Walls, 34.

CHAPTER 12: TO KILL A MOCKINGMOUSE OR SOMETHING FOR WIVES TO PASS TO THEIR HUSBANDS

Epigraphs:

Rudyard Kipling, "If," in *Rudyard Kipling*, ed. Eileen Gillooly (New York: Sterling Publishing, 2000), 21.
Elisabeth Elliot, *Mark of a Man* (Grand Rapids, MI: Revell, 1981), 153.
C. S. Lewis, *The Abolition of Man* (New York: HarperCollins, 2001), 26.

1. Studies vary with regard to our nation's divorce rate and other family-related statistics. These sources provide examples: "Marriage and Divorce," American Psychological Association, http://www.apa.org/topics/divorce/; "Births to Unmarried Women," Child Trends DataBank, http://www.childtrends.org/?indicators=births-to-unmarried-women /; and The AP, "Half of US Fathers Under 45 Have Child Out of Wedlock," *The National*, June 17, 2011—the article states that "nearly half" in this age category have "at least one child" born out of wedlock.
2. "Sara Leal: How Ashton Kutcher Seduced Me," *US Weekly*, October 11, 2011.
3. Nada Surf, *The Weight Is a Gift*, album for the Barsuk label (2005).
4. Ephesians 5:25.

CHAPTER 13: THE SOUND AND THE FURY

Epigraphs:

Paul the apostle, 2 Corinthians 1:6 (NLT).
Watchmen Nee cited in Martin H. Manser, comp., *The Westminster Collection of Christian Quotations* (Louisville: Westminster John Knox Press, 2001), 36.
Søren Kierkegaard et al., *Works of love* (New York: HarperPerennial, 2009), 77.

1. 2 Corinthians 1:3–4.

CHAPTER 14: OAK SHADOWS AND AUTUMN SUN

Epigraphs:

George Herbert, http://www.poetryfoundation.org/poem/181054.
Dr. Seuss, *I Can Read with My Eyes Shut!* (New York: Random House, 1978), 25.
George MacDonald cited in Martin H. Manser, comp., *The Westminster*

Collection of Christian Quotations (Louisville: Westminster John Knox Press, 2001), 62.

1. See Stephen King, "What Writing Is," in *On Writing* (New York: Simon and Schuster, 2002), 95–98.
2. Robert Frost cited in Edward C. Lathem and Lawrance Thompson, eds., *The Robert Frost Reader* (New York: Henry Holt, 1972), 381.
3. Isaiah 51:6.
4. 1 John 2:17.
5. Alister McGrath, *C. S. Lewis—A Life: Eccentric Genius, Reluctant Prophet* (Carol Stream, IL: Tyndale, 2013), 301.

DISCUSSION GUIDE

Epigraph:

William Nicholson, "Article written for The Daily Telegraph by William Nicholson at the time of publication," http://www.williamnicholson.com/2011/03/article-written-for-the-daily-telegraph-by-william-nicholson-at-the-time-of-publication/.

About the Authors

TIMOTHY WILLARD is an author, poet—though Jason simply says he's melodramatic—a blossoming rogue scholar, chaplain, and hack mountain biker. Nothing captures him like the quiet words of his wife, Chris, and the epiphanies of his three pixie daughters, Lyric, Brielle, and Zion. He feels like a farmer most days, plying the writing trade in the fields of imagination.

Though Timothy, like most writers, loves Hemingway, he does not understand why most writers fear using language. Given the choice between Joyce or Hemingway Timothy chooses the former. He abhors "ly" words even though he was forced to use them in this manuscript. To Timothy, writing is both a joy and an act of commitment. It is hard work, but refreshingly so.

Timothy coauthored *Veneer* and *Home Behind the Sun* and has collaborated on more than a dozen books with authors ranging from *New York Times* best sellers, platinum-selling and Grammy Award–winning artists, and former NFL MVPs. He is also finishing his first novel and children's book.

He serves as chaplain for the social entrepreneur accelerator program Praxis and has spoken at national conferences such as the Q Conference, Catalyst Conference, and Focus on the Family's Justice Conference.

Timothy holds a master's degree from Gordon-Conwell Theological Seminary and is reading for the PhD in theology at King's College London under the supervision of renowned theologian and apologist Alister McGrath.

* * *

JASON LOCY finds peace in the college memories of driving I-81 from Virginia to Pennsylvania to visit his future wife, Heather. During their sixteen years of marriage God has blessed them with a few trials and a few successes, all of which he's used to bring them closer together.

Every night he lies in bed and thanks God for his four incredible children, Ethan, Christian, Naomi, and Eliana. He then rolls over and asks God to keep them all asleep until morning.

When not wrangling the kids, Jason serves as creative director and principal of FiveStone, an award-winning branding and design firm he founded in 2001. FiveStone strives to move organizations from standard marketing hype to long-term sustainable strategies. The work there has garnered national and international attention.

With his friend Tim, Jason coauthored two books *Veneer* and *Home Behind the Sun*. Sometimes Jason speaks on the topics found in those books. Other times Jason is invited to speak on the principles of organizational storytelling or brand building.

Jason lives in Brooklyn, New York, where his slow Southern gait often keeps him from making the train.